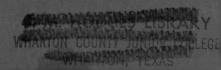

From the Housetops

From the Housetops

A Pastor Speaks to Adults

EDOUARD STEVENS

Translated by
MARY ILFORD

Introduction by
GERARD S. SLOYAN

HOLT, RINEHART AND WINSTON
NEW YORK   CHICAGO
SAN FRANCISCO

First Edition

Designer: Ernst Reichl
88144-0115
Printed in the United States of America

Contents

The Lord Speaks: The Liturgical Year

Advent

Christmas

Epiphany

Pentecost

The Lord Acts: The Signs of Love

From the Housetops

Introduction

Suppose the parish bulletins,
  mimeographed,
  that come in the mail,
  didn't dun you for
    bazaars,
    bizarres,
    A Fair Share,
but got you ready to hear the gospel
and were written outside the rectory,
outside the parish even, by
    Sean O'Faolain
      Muriel Spark
        Danilo Dolci
          John Updike
            Günter Grass
              all that crowd
who knew the Bible like the back of their hand.
  That would cause
        one hell of a fuss.

Sand in the gears
Imprimatur troubles
People going to other parishes
People (other people) *reading* the stuff.

Pretty rough on homilists, following an act like that.

But the people who kept coming to Mass,
who began to come to Mass
    to see if it was anything
    like the bulletin
would have open ears
                and a little hope.
Their first hope in a long time.

M. l'abbé Stevens is clever.
He's clever in French. He's clever in Glabais.   Pop. 510.
    He mightn't go over so big
    in Winesburg, Ohio
    Gibbsville, Pa.
But then, he doesn't have to.   He's in Glabais.

What's going on in those other parish bulletins,
mailings, handouts
        isn't
            very
                clever.

                Somebody has forgotten the gospel somewhere.

GERARD S. SLOYAN

Author's Preface

The texts presented here are not meant to be a synthesis of the liturgical year, or even of material for sermons.

They were posted inside or in front of the church, or mimeographed and circulated to the houses in the parish, only as preparation for the next sermon. Their purpose was thus to arouse or direct the attention rather than to nourish it.

That is why they do not touch on the central themes of the faith, remaining deliberately peripheral, as a question might to the answer.

The Christian mystery can then be proposed in its own framework of time, place, gesture, language, and symbolism, where it encounters the instructed—or the instructible. The richness of the faith is revealed and nurtured only in the "desert" of the Church and the liturgy.

Hence these papers do not form a homogenous whole. If, for example, Christ is often referred to as the "New Man," it is not mentioned, or only rarely, that he is first of all the Son of God, that being the subject and foundation of the sermon itself.

Then again, some passages may appear unduly hard on the indifferent, or on the non-practicing who ask for church weddings or baptisms. Groups and areas certainly exist where the indifference of these non-practicing Catholics conceals vestiges of a genuine and living faith, which cannot be treated with blind severity. Nevertheless, experience here has shown that pastoral severity, clearly enunciated and explained, tends to revive, rather than destroy, such vestiges of faith.

Another point. Some expressions, some analogies, a certain familiar tone, certain liberties of language, of grammar, or of style, may be justified in a particular environment and within the limits of a clearly defined literary style. In another environment and in the context of another literary style, they would be out of place.

For instance, we can speak of Christ as the boss of the plant only where people use it as a term of respect, where they see dignity in labor, in the solidarity which unites workers and boss on the job for the good of the job, where the term is current not only in everyday speech but also in the honest and accepted language of labor. It then implies a decent familiarity, made up of respect for each man's task, and for each man in the performance of his task. To speak of Christ as boss in other literary forms such as sermons, Bible readings, or prayers would be out of place, for these have their own conventions.

GLABAIS, April 1963   E. STEVENS

By Way of Beginning

Believers are people who
choose to believe
> that a pinnacle exists which is higher than
> matter,
> with its time, its distances, its changes.

Christians are people who
choose to follow
> a school, a method, a master,
> in order to find, serve, announce, and intro-
> duce the God
> of the Jews, of Jesus, of the Church.

Hence, Christians,
> in order to become
> the effective heralds of their God,
> the effective servants of his plans,
> the effective beneficiaries of his rewards,
study
> Judaism, Christ, and Christianity,
and train
> in the various services of the God
> of holiness, of unity, of joy
> (and no one has ever claimed this was easy) .

For Christians,
> matter is a springboard,
> the universe a field to be reclaimed and de-
> veloped,
> the Church a caravan in transit,

unbelievers are younger brothers who have to
be awakened,
Mass is a gathering around the leader,
and the rest of the time is *doing*.

For unbelievers,
all this is a lot of idle talk, and it annoys them.
It makes sense only for priests, the rich, or the
respectable,
who are scared of getting tired, or dirty, or
of enjoying themselves.

Then there is a third man,
the non-practicing believer.
Is he an executioner, a victim,
a gate-crasher, a child, a criminal, an invalid?
Who shall say?
What matters now is not whether he mends
his ways.
But at least let him know how his brothers see him:

He is the man who
goes away when others come rushing up to
learn,
sleeps while others watch,
disappears when others fight,
dances when others suffer,
makes money when others are training,
has himself carried by those who go on foot.

This third man
    is as precious to us
    as Christ and as ourselves.

This whole book
    is written for him.
    To get him to say something.

Do you hear?
    Even your anger
    would be better than your silence—
    the silence of the absent.

The Lord Speaks

The Liturgical Year

Advent

First Sunday

> . . . it is now the hour for us
> to rise from sleep.
>
> EPISTLE

Through Advent, we shall go up
to Christmas.
And from Christmas to Easter, Jesus will reveal to us
the new world which his Father offers him.
And those who take their faith seriously
begin right now to make ready for Easter
in the Church.

We have to have a good knowledge of man (Adam)
to understand the Son of man (Christ).
We must have suffered greatly at being
no more than we are
to rejoice in Christ.

What we are? What every man is?
a stranger to himself and to others, despising himself and
    believing himself despised;
a phonograph grinding out impossible demands, wild de-
    sires;

a wrangler, jealous of everything, satisfied with nothing;
a coward who struts when the enemy is far;
a solitary hedgehog which pricks because it believes another is pricking it;
a blind man, prattling about all he thinks he sees;
an awkward toddler, alone and foolish in his playpen, who wants to be treated like a grown-up;
someone who is always trying, starting over again, failing, and again starting. And then dies.
A failure . . . No: the valiant builder of the future—of what *is to come.*

But the Man who is to come has come. *He is coming.*
You are cooperating in his coming.

Christ
is man's access to his own humanity;
the passage from childhood to maturity;
the emergence from sin to oneness;
the goodness in what is incomplete leading to the peace of fulfillment;
everything and everyone for each of us;
sovereignty in us and over the rest.

For 600 centuries, Adam was *becoming*—laboriously.
For 20 centuries, Christ has been *coming*—victoriously.
Humanity is *coming* victoriously:
purified, fulfilled, kneaded, judged, acquitted, glorified, unified, grafted on Christ.

Twentieth-century man, you have only to pass through the "door" to find yourself in the new man, the Kingdom, the new world which 600,000 years of toil have built for you, for us. The feast is waiting for you . . .

You don't want to go to it

Yes, you do. You do want to, because otherwise you
     wouldn't be here.
Come, take your place beside the judge, beside the judges.
Sit next to the King. Take the robe he's holding out to you.
Seize the crown he offers you; he paid for it very dearly.
Adopt his style, his manners.
With, in, through, and like him, rule and reign.
Rule yourself and the world.
Don't let the field you are, the field you have, lie fallow.
Don't turn away from one who is more You than you are.
With him you are sure to reach the summit; God awaits
you there.

Everything he did is for you, now that you're an adult.
Christ thought of no one else but you when he did what
he did.
He came for you. And now let him come through you.

Advent

Second Sunday

The Gentiles, in him, shall find hope.
EPISTLE

The nations are about to emerge from their nationalism.
The eggshell is ready to crack.
God is about to speak, as a ruler.

Through man, human lordship will arise, the product of a testing plant that has long been at work. That workshop is the Jewish people, and then Mary.

God creates a new man, a whole man, by a new spirit.

Compared with the New Testament, the Old Law is a prison (John the Baptist's). Obedience without sharing the spirit of one's leader is slavery.

Advent

Third Sunday

> Say to the fainthearted, "Take courage and
> fear not. Behold, our God will come and will
> save us."
> COMMUNION

You, Christian,
are the worker who knows the Master.

He adopts you as his only son
and heir to all he possesses.
With him
you can create
your own universe of glory and peace.

Give him
your person,
your children,
your time,
your ears,
your trust,
your good qualities,
your failings,
your neighbors,
your surroundings,
the short span of your life . . .

You received it from him.

All the rest
you will find
in him.
He comes to you.
Go, now, to him.
You are not a stone
or a plant
or an animal.
You are his son
and he gives you
a world to build:

"You have favored, O Lord, your land;
you have restored the well-being of Jacob.
You have forgiven the guilt of your people;
you have covered all their sins.
You have withdrawn all your wrath;
you have revoked your burning anger.

Restore us, O God our Saviour,
and abandon your displeasure against us.
Will you be ever angry with us,
prolonging your anger to all generations?
Will you not instead give us life;
and shall not your people rejoice in you?
Show us, O Lord, your kindness,
and grant us your salvation.

I will hear what God proclaims;
the Lord—for he proclaims peace

to his people, and to his faithful ones,
and to those who put in him their hope.
Near indeed is his salvation to those who fear him,
glory dwelling in our land.
Kindness and truth shall meet;
justice and peace shall kiss.
Truth shall spring out of the earth,
and justice shall look down from heaven.
The Lord himself will give his benefits;
our land shall yield its increase.
Justice shall walk before him,
and salvation, along the way of his steps."

(Psalm 84)

Why not say this psalm together as a family evening prayer? A Christian family is not just like any other family. It is not just a community as regards food, board, TV, roof, recreation, quarrels, sufferings, budget, experience.

It is also a community united in thanksgiving, in gratitude, in prayer, in divine responsibility, in joy, like the branches of a tree around their trunk, Christ.

Advent

Fourth Sunday

> The voice of one crying in the desert,
> "Make ready the way of the Lord,
> make straight his paths . . ."
> GOSPEL

Why the desert?

John the Baptist,
Mary,
Joseph,
are three figures of the desert.

John, by his mode of life;
Mary, by her virginity (virgin soil is empty, clean, ready to receive seed);
Joseph, son of David, without a kingdom and without progeny.

These three figures gave us Christmas.
There is no other way of gaining Christmas.
Like them, we shall receive Jesus, we shall "watch over" Jesus, we shall proclaim Jesus through everything in us.

How can we make our desert?

By cleaning, spring-cleaning, house-cleaning: making room for God.
Listening to him and not to our instincts.

Caring about him instead of dwelling on our own little
   cares.
Giving him our time instead of taking up his.

Then . . . Christmas will come.

Then, poor as we are, we shall receive the power of God,
like Mary; the power to bring forth a Son of God, the
power to become a son of God, the power to make another
Christ of ourselves, and to show this miracle to everyone.

Christianity does not say that God exists. That is something all religions know.

Christianity says:
that this God is incarnate;
that he continues to become incarnate in as
many faces as there are human beings;
that every Christian is Christ,
and that this is evident from our actions.

Christmas

Christmas Eve

O Almighty God, we eagerly look forward
to the adorable birthday of your Son;
grant that we may also receive
his everlasting gifts with joy . . .
SECRET

When a child becomes an adolescent, he opens his eyes.
And everything seems to be all right. Everything, save for
one small matter (and this is his first personal religious
discovery, his first spiritual exam, or test, or contest):

He does wrong, and he hurts,
when he doesn't want to;
he doesn't do right, he doesn't do good,
when he would like to.

Now he knows that evil (committed or suffered) has its
roots in him: it's a fact. Evil has a foothold in him. Now he
can no longer indulge in the luxury of judging others as
though he were perfect himself. Evil has an emissary in his
heart as in his body. It's very strange and very disappointing. It's outrageous: I buy a loaf of bread . . . and it's
moldy. I receive this wonderful life from my parents . . .
and it's rotten, it leads to wickedness and suffering and

death. . . . So what's the score, finally? And he tells himself: insofar as goodness is concerned, and faith, and Christ, and generosity, and purity, and work, and fellowship—I make a pretty *poor* showing . . .

Now he stands at the parting of the ways:
He can forget; or he can admit to the facts.

He can *forget* his faults as you throw away a scrap of paper, as you mend a tear.

But the scar remains—a feeling of shame, like a wisp of smoke, light but tenacious, a reminder that there, and still there, a fire broke out at one time. . . . It's awkward. What else is to be done?

He loses some of his lightheartedness, some of his high spirits, some of his youthfulness of mind and heart and inclination—inclination for work, for play, for service, for friends, for parents, for simple pleasures.

Then he finds the solution: a *mask*. He acts "as if." A polite smile takes the place of a joyous one. Pointless diversions take the place of the fresh and friendly pleasures he used to enjoy. He becomes harsh in his talk, both with his parents and his former friends.

But now, all of a sudden, he finds himself very much alone, helpless, disgusted with himself. And beneath the mask, the rats of "evil" get on with their little job, undisturbed. In short, he realizes that the evil he does is also an evil he suffers.

This is the same awareness we find in the great prophets of Israel.

Is there another way of combating evil which does not lead to isolation?

Yes, by *confessing* the evil, as the Advent saints put it, and then *being converted*. These two things make up a single act, and they are a sure remedy.

Conversion is a long, hard, astonishing, exciting process. But that's why we are here on earth, why we are men and responsible for our own actions (like gods). Our job, as sons of God, is to complete the world of men. God makes us partners in his "business."

Confession and conversion—that is Christ's solution. And his reason for coming among us was to take on this vast job along with us. He wants to get us to become his equals, his brothers, his fellow workers, his fellow creators, his "spit and image."

His friends are the millions of adolescents that we all are. He is the leader of the expedition for the liberation of the territory of mankind. Its spiritual liberation.

Fear nothing, he says. Come on, you over there! I'm coming too. The climb is not too steep for you. I know, everyone knows, and you know that you're starting very far down, in darkness and weakness and obscurity. All men start that way. It's the way I started, just like you. Come. I am coming. We'll see each other soon. I'm in as great a hurry as you. But you're climbing. You're climbing to glory, my glory.

Give me your hand. . . . Thank you.
Give me your ears. . . . Thank you.
Give me your tongue. . . . Thank you.
Give me your feet. . . . Thank you.
Give me your time. . . . Thank you.
Stand over here with the rest.
Keep together. Trust me.
And forward, through the desert.

You see? Things are all right now. And you have found
    youthfulness and joy again, and all the rest.
The first step toward me is *confession*.
The second is *conversion*.
The third, you'll see tomorrow . . . You already see the
    light returning: within us, within men,
O men, my stars.

Christmas

Amid the brightness of the saints,
before the daystar was made, I have
begotten you.

COMMUNION

God is the only friend you treat like a dog.
You need him? . . . You whistle for him.
It's Sunday? . . . You throw him a half-hour,
like a bone.
He's in your way? . . . You shove him aside.
He asks for your friendship? . . . You toss him a dime.
He calls you to work? . . . You rush off
to the bar, or the movies, or the TV . . .
He's explaining his plans? . . . You watch
the clock.

Is that what you were baptized for?
No!

Your parents and godparents swore, on their honor,
and by their immortal souls, to initiate you, by example
and by word, in Christ's ways.

When they tossed you into the water, you were still un-
formed. They brought you out, stamped clearly with his
image, and they urged you to get to work in the Church of
Christ, their friend.

It's on their behalf that I speak to you.

If you are of Christ, celebrate Christmas by having Christ come into your life, into your conduct.

If you want to deny your baptism, don't celebrate Christmas at all, for you will only make yourself ridiculous in everyone's eyes. You might do better to celebrate the winter solstice, which heralds summer and brings the springtime.

Christmas is *Christ*mas:

The only evil, the only pain, and the only struggle of a man whose conscience begins to awaken is the daily experience of weakness and loneliness, with no one waiting for him, no one hearing him, no one serving him.

But by means of work, the arts, the sciences, technology, religion—and patience, those that have been awakened arouse, encourage, and organize the sluggards who come late, or who have gone back to sleep.

Whether known or not, whether recognized or not, Christ is the leader and the first of those who are awake.

Christmas is when he comes, like the morning sun, and shouts to us—and makes us shout: Get up. Wash yourselves. There's work to do in the Kingdom of God.

I am Christ, the Messias, the Son of Man, the Son of God, the Servant of God and the King of the world.

At home, in heaven, the greatest is the servant of his friends, his juniors, his guests.

I serve. Serve as I do. We shall reign together.

I have received all things from my Father:
all is mine. And I give it all to you.

Epiphany

O God, who by the star this day revealed
your only-begotten Son to all nations,
grant that we, who know you now by
faith, may be brought one day before
the vision of your majesty.

PRAYER

You, too, are one of the Wise Men. Yes, even you.

For you know that you should be richer, stronger, happier, more intelligent. You know that we are certainly not here on earth just to sleep, eat, work, sleep again, eat again, work again, and to go through all this in struggle, in pain, in loneliness, in sickness, in death—with just enough leisure to bring kids into the world, who will sleep, eat, and work in their turn, from the days of their youthful hopes to the inevitable frustration of death, the final disappointment.

You know there is more to it than that. But what?

Suppose, for instance, the children could be a little better off than you? Suppose that in two, three, or four generations, they could all lead really comfortable lives? Right away you would begin to find your hard life a little more worth living.

At heart, you really do believe that things will turn out like that. It's because of this you haven't hanged yourself yet, along with your wife and children.

At heart, you believe that life must become different from what it is, and that it will.

You believe that one day man will be a king—happy, good, rich, and joyful.

You believe that today's work is only a steppingstone to that triumph.

But the point is that the Wise Men were already intelligent enough to believe all this. This light was already in their minds and hearts. If, nevertheless, they continued to walk in the night and in the desert of the world, it was because they were ambitious, people who were determined to get someplace, who were not satisfied with half-lights.

The Wise Men who arrived in Bethlehem were very lucky. They happened on the very person who was to be, in a complete way, their light, their health, their life, and their joy. They happened on the only man who could act as their model, their fuel, their pilot, their guide, their shepherd, their road, their beacon, and their fortress, who could be all these things for all who met him, sought him, listened to him, followed him, and believed in him completely.

They knew that their taste for happiness was nothing but the spirit of God germinating in them. They knew that the purpose of their earthly journey was nothing less than to become a new man, in whom that spirit had reached maturity and become fully operative.

And they knew that Jesus was there simply to bring them what they lacked.

Today's wise men are those who are willing to emerge from their shells to draw nearer to Christ. Their backsides are not glued to their easy chairs, their eyes to the TV screen, their hearts to the past. They dare to ask around them where they might find Christ. They are not put off because the road is long or badly lit. They are not shocked at being welcomed every Sunday by a small child of insignificant appearance. . . .

And they know that the Church is only the lamp which holds that light. After each weekly encounter with Christ, they at once go home, each a bit more of a child-king, a child-God, and they pass on some of their divine luster to others, to those others who seek it. And one day everyone will possess it.

So be a *wise man,* intelligent and anxious to be still more so. As the one who possesses it for that divine luster. Then nourish it, spread it.

One day, thanks to you, the world will be one vast celestial power station, a great star of glory among God's other stars—the greatest of my stars, says Jesus, the glorious body of God the Son. It was that mysterious figure, born of God and of a daughter of Jacob, bearer of the royal name of the Jewish kings—ben-David, Davidson, "son of David"— who let himself be killed by fools in order to live within the "wise," and to make of these his eternal people, his guests at the banquet of life.

Your time on earth, dear wise man, is but the time to prepare for your feast. And tomorrow, in the house of God our Father, you will celebrate your feast, our feast.

For life can only be a feast. A boundless one, in every sense.

The Holy Family

> The parents of Jesus took him up to
> Jerusalem to present him to the Lord.
> OFFERTORY

What is this ardent, radiant life that Christ brings to the
world? What is our life as Christians, our life as Christ's
successors, Christ's representatives, Christ's members?

Everything starts with a radical change, so radical that
it is called sacrifice and death. The past is left behind,
with its habits and its idols; you place yourself at God's
disposal; you die "to the flesh," as the Scripture says.

The assembly of the faithful make this gesture at the
Offertory, as Mary and Joseph did when they presented
their son in the Temple. After all, to offer one's self, or to
offer one's son, comes to the same thing; my son is what-
I-make-of-myself, my production, my word, myself-for-
others, the giving of myself.

For Mary and Joseph, the sacrificial aspect of this hand-
ing over to God was particularly acute: Jesus stayed behind in the Temple, attending to his Father's business . . .

That business is not *ours*.

God's business is not men's business.

God's will is not men's will.

God's logic is not men's logic.

The Christian's home is not the house of his
natural parents.

For us, who are baptized, the natural family is
a pagan, outworn notion. (Matt. 12:46–50; Luke, 11:27–28)

34

The Christian does not live enclosed in a cozy, comfortable little nest. The Christian family is one that has burst open, wide open, that has gone into the service of the Father, the universal Father.

Christian families are the family of Christians, which extends to the whole parish and the whole Church.

So there is a breach, a separation, a passage from one family to another, from one house (Nazareth) to another (the Temple), from one life to another, from the service of our thousand little gods (money, vacations, children, studies, career, success, comfort, TV, car, position . . .) to the service of the one true God, the one living God.

Once this passage has been achieved, once we have placed our persons, our actions, our sons, at the service of God, God takes possession of us and sends us back into the world—as witnesses, as sons of God, as other Christs.

At the *Ite, missa est,* the Christian leaves the temple and returns into the world, to his village, to his family (as Jesus returned to Nazareth). He now has a divine calling (which St. Paul describes in Colossians 3:12–17): to proclaim that he belongs to God by his whole attitude, by his every word and action, by a joyous, eager, productive life, perfectly attuned to circumstances (for instance, perfect subjection to his superiors, like Jesus at Nazareth), a life that shows all who observe him what kind of man the living God produces.

Epiphany

Second Sunday

> But thou hast kept the good wine
> until now.
>
> GOSPEL

Who is Jesus, anyway? A script writer, a poet, a doctor,
a bonesetter, a magician, a missionary, a politician, an agi-
tator, a ringleader, one of the unemployed?

Prior to Cana (in the twenty Masses of the Christmas
season), he allows himself to be introduced by a whole
series of officials of all ranks: John the Baptist, Mary,
Joseph, Zachary, Elizabeth, the shepherds, the Wise Men,
the angels, Simeon, Anna, the doctors of the university of
Jerusalem, Herod.

Today, at Cana, on the second Sunday after the Epiph-
any, he takes up his duties, magisterially inaugurating his
life's work. He announces the full scope of his plans and
of the mission he intends to assume.

Mary, first, and then the Twelve, watch it all; they understand and decide to go along.

What does it so clearly mean to them, this meal which
came so close to going wrong?

The world is starving, he says. But the owner has sent
me as his steward to bring about prosperity. Let him who
loves me follow me.

Mary and the Twelve understand, because they remember all that has been recorded in the Scriptures:

Isaia The wine is sour. There are no more village fairs. There's no more music. The merriest are groaning. The clarinets are stowed away. The sound of rejoicing has faded.

Osee No one comes to drink wine and eat sweet cakes at Yahweh's house for the feast of the fathers. . . . Let them drink mud.

Amos The mountains and the hills will run with new wine.

Joel The dried-up streams will bubble with sweet water, the barns will be bursting with wheat and the cellars with the best wine.

Jeremia All the people will flock to my city and will find new bread, the best wine, and meat to their hearts' content. The heart of my people will be as gay as a garden that has had all the rain and sun it needs. They will no longer languish like prisoners or slaves, far from their Father's house.

Osee They will come back to sit in my shadow. They will work their fields and tend their vineyards again with profit, making them the best in the world. Every day, at every meal, they will drink the finest wine.

Isaia In his city (Church), God is preparing a feast of juicy meats and full-bodied wines for all the peoples of the world.

Canticle of Canticles Eat your fill, my friends, and drink deep. Here is my new wine and my freshly baked bread.

The people in Cana must also remember the story of Joseph in Egypt:

Genesis Famine reigned throughout the world. Then Pharao said: "Go to Joseph and do what he tells you." (Mary will later remind us of this.) And "Joseph opened all the storehouses." (Jesus was to echo these words.)

Genesis Pharao said to Joseph (and his charge was to be repeated by God the Father, Mary, and Jesus): "You shall be in charge of my palace, and all my people shall obey your commands; only as regards the royal throne will I be greater than you. . . ." Joseph was thirty years old. He left Pharao and traversed the whole land of Egypt (Jesus after his baptism).

Exodus Then Pharao worked wonders in the sight of the people. The people were won over and praised God for deigning to care for them through the agency of a man. (The Evangelist plays on these words.)

John the Baptist, too, plays on words: "I have seen and have borne witness that this is the Son of God." (Servant of Pharao, Joseph.)

Mary, who now understands, cries out in her joy: "Do whatever he tells you."

The Father, too, joins in. From heaven, he proclaims: "This is my beloved Son, in whom I am well pleased. Hear him."

Clearly, they all recall the old story of Joseph, sold by his brothers, and saving both them and the Egyptians from famine. . . .

And now, as for us, shall we eat this new bread? Or not?
And shall we come to listen to what he says? Or not?
And shall we do what he asks? Or not?
It's up to you now, my brothers.

Epiphany

Third Sunday

> Amen I say to you, I have not found such
> great faith in Israel.
>
> GOSPEL

The Church is speaking of itself and of us, here,
this morning.

A short play in two scenes.

Setting
On the horizon, a high mountain, the Temple.
On the left, a path leading to the Temple.
On the right, a path leading to Capharnaum.
The roof of a house.
A crossroads where three paths meet.

Characters
Christ.
The Jews who follow him.
The Jews who don't follow him (the absentees).
A Jewish leper (excommunicated).
A pagan whose servant is sick (not on the job).

Action
Two confessions, humble appeals for mercy.
Two answers, prompt and efficacious.
A twinge: the pagans are there, . . . a whole lot of Jews
are giving me the cold shoulder.

Here, as in a Mass, we recognize the three classical stages of the spiritual life:

1. The going up. A public, reckless commitment—
   the Jew might be punished for breaking the law;
   the Roman makes himself ridiculous in the eyes of the Romans.
2. The offering. An admission of weakness and an appeal to Christ: words and actions.
3. The answer, spoken and fulfilled—
   to the Jew: he is publicly, officially, ordered to return to the service of the chosen people;
   to the pagan: a promise that he will be met on his own ground.

In Jesus:
delight at the trust placed in him;
pain at the stubborn hostility of his kin.

Our community, part present, part absent, arouses the same reactions in Jesus: "Go thy way; as thou hast believed, so be it done to thee," he says. As for the sons of the kingdom, they "will be put forth into the darkness outside."

Epiphany

Fourth Sunday

> The right hand of the Lord has exercised power;
> the right hand of the Lord has lifted me up.
>
> OFFERTORY

"Then Jesus got into a boat." After doing what? After waking up twelve men who were following him. After drawing them out of childhood, chaos, nothingness.

Jesus does the same thing on Septuagesima Sunday. He comes to rouse us from sleep and put us to work. Septuagesima is the first peal of the Easter bells.

Eve also was brought out of Adam as he slept. Eve is the aspect of man awakening to a new world, becoming aware of a new facet of the world and of himself: the wealth of this world and the possibility of having children, of achieving boundless divine happiness.

Meanwhile, Adam sleeps; he is kept "in reserve" for another enlightenment, the ultimate awakening of mankind: that of Christ and of "other Christs."

Christ, therefore, awakens twelve men, a crew, *all of us here present*. . . .

And to make it perfectly clear that he has mastered chaos, he sets out upon the water, sovereign ruler of the barrenness of the waters, that symbol of inveterate sleep. A terrible storm arises suddenly. Let it rage—chaos will be overcome. The forces of chaos (negative) and the forces of God (positive) are governed by the Son of Man, by our whole world!

The Church is at its most resplendent, spiritually, when things are at their worst according to the flesh. Never is it so triumphant over the world as when it is persecuted. That being so, remember, Christians, that the hard knocks you get are to teach you to build this world which you are called upon to rule.

For it is your job to build it by awakening your sleeping younger brothers. And it's urgent. We have no more than seventy or eighty years to spend on earth. We must use this short time to rouse them from their childishness.

A practical application: At ten, or twelve, children are geniuses as regards religion. Most of them! Then it fades. It is at that point that parents must become fully aware of their responsibility.

Epiphany

Fifth Sunday

> But gather the wheat into
> my barn.
> GOSPEL

The clergy (disciples) go into a village to make everything
ready for him.
But the people won't have him
because
he is on his way to Jerusalem.

The clergy suggest calling down fire from heaven to con-
sume the Samaritans.
Turning, Jesus reprimands them.

At another time, he speaks of awaiting the harvest
to separate the wheat from the weeds.

(A wink.)

Epiphany

Sixth Sunday

> The kingdom of heaven is like a grain
> of mustard seed . . .
> the birds of the air come and dwell
> in its branches.
>
> GOSPEL

Creation is growth.
Growth is a leap from one pole to the other on the same
    axis.

At one end, the least,
at the other, the most:

child	–	old man
call	–	answer
chaos	–	mind
Adam	–	Christ
disciple	–	doctor
slave	–	king
virgin	–	mother
night	–	day
sea	–	mountain
seed	–	tree bearing fruits and birds
dough	–	bread

Septuagesima

First stage of the ascent to Easter

The *Septuagesima* readings throw light on the fact of our existence, of our being here. We are here because we have been called. We have been called to work like laborers, to work in Christ's vineyard for a perfect wage, the same for all.

Sexagesima goes into the problems of this work. We have been at it since Adam, and problems arise because not everything in us and around us is ready and willing to accept the Word (seed) which will make it possible for the work to produce its results (fruits).

Quinquagesima announces the outcome of a job well done, the apotheosis at the summit of the Lenten climb: the everlasting light of the Spirit to which we are called to enter.

So during three Sundays we shall build a threefold liturgical portal to Eastertide:
1. The call, or creation, by the Father. (The Father launches the undertaking.)
2. Work, the Son's achievement. (The Son carries out the undertaking.)

3. Eschatology. (The Spirit crowns it all.)
From our point of view this means:
to be there—to do—to enjoy;
to come—to answer—to receive;
to be appointed—to exercise—to be rewarded;
to take up arms—to hold the front—to parade through the
    capital.

Thus three solemn chords joyously inaugurate the Lenten season. And in these chords are harmonized the themes which will be developed in depth at each successive stage of the journey.

Septuagesima:	call	*to come*
Sexagesima:	instruction	*to learn*
Quinquagesima:	reward	*to enjoy*

These first three of the seventy-four steps leading to Easter sum up all history, all faith, our whole life, and outline the work we are to undertake with the catechumens to show them what kind of feast they are invited to.
1. God calls you and appoints you "directors" of his creation.
2. Then he initiates you in this craft:
he cries out his Word to you, and at first you feel like spitting it out, vomiting it . . . but then you start chewing on it after all, and in the end you swallow a few mouthfuls.
3. That will be the day of triumph.

It starts today. Easter starts today.

Septuagesima

> The moaning of death surrounded me, the
> sorrows of hell enveloped me. In my distress
> I called upon the Lord, and he heard my voice.
> INTROIT

Only seventy days to Easter, now. Like the seventy years
exile in Babylon. During those seventy days, and even during these three weeks before Lent, we are going to study
and live like the exiles of the Babylonian captivity who
tried not to be absorbed into the society around them. We
shall live the exile of those who wait and do not possess.
We shall live this suffering and this hope.

Introit
The first thing to do is to cry out to the Lord.

It's to him we must turn, and not elsewhere. A child who
is in trouble goes to his parents.

Epistle
St. Paul considers two problems: how should we work,
and what wages will we get in the end?

This is no time for sleeping. We shall rest later. Now we
have to flex our muscles and pull with all our strength, as
in a contest. And each of us must act as if he alone could
win. As for the victor's wreath, it will not be of laurel, to
be tossed out with the garbage a month later; it will be
enduring.

The Israelites did not all win the prize either. Even
though all had been led by the cloud—which both blinds

and illuminates, in which God both reveals and conceals himself—that is, all had lived in a godly environment, in a religious atmosphere, with catechism, Sunday Mass, and so on; and even though all had crossed the Red Sea (had been baptized, says St. Paul), very few were found pleasing to God, not even Moses. (This to make it quite clear that Moses is not the final figure to be awaited.) Only two won approval: Caleb and Josue, the only ones not to balk at the difficulties presented by the conquest of the Promised Land—an impossible undertaking, of course, but one commanded by Yahweh (like the crossing of the Red Sea) and therefore assured of success.

Gradual

These verses exactly define what the Hebrews needed to get out of the desert immediately, instead of wandering in it for forty years. To trust God, we must know him. To find him, we must seek him. If we don't seek him, there is nothing anyone can do to help us. The "poor man" is the man who seeks God because he is not content with man. His poverty goads him on to seek.

Lord, don't let what's purely human in me get the upper hand! Take it away, get rid of whatever's in your way!

Tract

I've done plenty of damage, Lord, but I won't do any more. And you can always patch it up, after all.

We ask God not to take our sins into account. St. Paul asks Christians to remember this in their dealings with each other.

Next, the Psalmist speaks of promises. We must therefore know what they are.

God's justice will be to fulfill his promises to the letter. He does what he says: that is his privilege. There is no parallel to that in our world: the harvest does not fulfill the promise of the sowing, the fruit that of the flower, the adult that of the child. And yet the promise was there. Only God never lets us down.

Gospel

Who are you? Why do you lie there sleeping? Why do you act like the baby who goes on lying in his crib after he is supposed to climb out?

We have acted like babies in regard to God, but we are called upon to grow up and to produce. That is Christ's message to us as he comes very early in the morning (that is, with the rising of the sun, that symbol of a king or a divinity revealing himself) to meet the laborers.

Every man is necessarily a laborer. But for all that, Christ, when he comes, must find men who are not working for another boss (money, girls, their bellies). If they are employed elsewhere, then Christ finds no one. They are driven by some power other than a taste for Christ. It's useless, then, to preach to them; they would miss the whole point of the preaching.

So there are three conditions to be fulfilled: not to be otherwise employed, to feel we were made to work, and to be unhappy that no one wants to bother with us.

Then the Word will come, the true sun and the true glory. He will come at every hour of the day to ask us to join him. And each will receive the same wage: life and the Holy Spirit, which are indeed inseparable, just like the presence of Christ. Once you know him, see him, once you are his friend, how boundless the marvel of it! Just as the last paschal candle you light burns as brightly as the first, so all the children in a family receive the same love from their parents.

The evening, here, stands for the end of the world. The latecomers are ourselves (like the prodigal son). The only firstcomer is Christ—but that's no problem, since he is the servant of the rest. As for those who think they were there from the start, and protest, insisting on their rights, Christ gives them a good lesson on the subject of the distribution of rewards, goods, and salaries. He seizes one by the scruff of his neck and tells him that he gives as he pleases. "Or art thou envious because I am generous?"

You have to be a pretty miserable character to act like that egotist. And yet it's very common, it happens all the time, and it blocks all kinds of things. Give a rag to a poor man, and all the others will protest and say it's unfair!

What Jesus is doing here is dilating hearts. The first (he who has been working in his Father's garden from all eternity) will indeed be the last; we shall be served before him and by him. The called are all those who are present at the start of the Lenten climb; the chosen are those who reach the top, who come out into the light and penetrate the Spirit of God.

Offertory

When you believe, it's a joy to proclaim your faith.

To sing the glory of God is what real *being* is, overflowing with life, glowing with health. A healthy child rejoices in his parents; an unruly one doesn't. It is up to us to mold ourselves, with God's help. For we are not very strong, but he is powerful, and he is our Father.

And what luck to have such a Father!

Sexagesima

The seed is the word of God.
GOSPEL

Christians, in sixty days it will be Easter.
Last week, we crossed the threshold into Eastertide.
That threshold was made up of two parts:
one, recalling the creation, the call, man's appointment
to paradise to take up his noble task (Septuagesima);
the other, pointing to the paschal triumph, the passage
of our flesh to divine glory (Candlemas).
So it really is Christ who has called us, gathered us here,
this morning.
If he is to make "other Christs" of us, he must instruct
us, train us. Even a prince has to learn his princely duties.

School
The time between now and the liturgical Easter (or the
real Easter of our death) is a school: a traveling school,
like a training ship. We take to the road together, and we
go through our life on earth like a caravan through a desert, without isolating ourselves or fooling with mirages or
getting excited about trifles. What we have to do is listen
to our guide, Jesus, and do what he says.
And it's no easier than any other real schooling. You
don't learn how to act like "another Christ" in a couple of
hours, or in a couple of years of catechism, or by imitating
your neighbors, or by secretly studying other, easier sub-
jects which seem likely to yield more immediate profits, or
. . . or . . . or . . .

That is what Jesus is telling us today: there are all sorts in our school, including those who flunk out.

There's the type who just vegetates on the shores of faith. He doesn't work; his body is here, but not his energy, his heart, his intelligence, his memory, his imagination. As soon as I turn my back, says Jesus, he takes off and starts playing around with my enemies (the wayside).

Then there's the type who walks out indignantly at the first setback. He's trying to find the living God and at the same time cultivate the two kinds of death (the thorns).

But it is not only this petty and frivolous type who will flunk. There is also the incurably proud man, the "me, me," the "I, I" (the rocks), who withers alone and empty, convinced that if he does something wrong it's always someone else's fault, that he's the victim.

But there's also the good man (the good soil), who grows his roots deep, who lifts up his branches, who patiently builds himself and builds the Kingdom, who does the necessary chores and does them pleasantly, quietly, efficiently, correcting his own faults bit by bit, waiting patiently and eagerly to see what the master of the school tells his students. He's there, with eyes and ears wide open, and his hands and feet ready too. If he's called on, he answers, and he comes.

He doesn't ask just to be coddled and coaxed and spoiled and entertained, and, for heaven's sake, to be left alone! He's a worker, a man. He can be turned into a Christ, into a shining light, radiating God's glory like the head of his school, Jesus, the first Christ. He advances from week to week because he seeks, because he doesn't invent a thousand excuses to refuse the Word and the sacraments.

Some will take Lent seriously, with its gatherings (Wednesdays, Fridays, Sundays), its tools (frequent Communion, self-amendment, penance).

They will reach the top of the arid slopes of Sinai and Jerusalem and thence will gaze on the vast horizon of light they have conquered.

Christian, your Easter depends on the forty-times-twenty-four hours of your Lent. And your Easter is not just the liturgical celebration on Holy Saturday night.

Your Easter is your death: will you make of it a birth in God, as a son, as another Christ?

You, there, are you going to pick up your cards and play, or not?

Quinquagesima

What wouldst thou have me
do for thee?
GOSPEL

If you're coming up with us, only fifty days more, and it will really be Easter.

Septuagesima celebrated our hiring by Christ.

Sexagesima celebrated the job he gave us to do: to sow and cultivate the soil in which the seed of his Word is growing.

Quinquagesima celebrates our good fortune in being able to work for him, the only boss who harvests the Spirit of God (that wisdom which tempted Eve) and who shares all the profits with his workers.

The Gospel shows him in the thick of the action:

He proposes to go up to Jerusalem, to be killed there.

He proposes to defy death, to break its power, and to transform it into the bridge to heaven.

He proposes to take his disciples along, to let them see with their own eyes, to toughen them by having them witness his struggle, his method, his triumph.

And before starting off, he tells them (lesson of the blind man cured) that he is able to communicate his fire, his light, his power, to anyone who will listen to him, ask him, and follow him.

His program: to make humanity happy, rich, and immortal. That is the purpose of God's creation and man's toil.

His terms: that we realize that the effort required is colossal, indeed impossible without him; that he can form and transform us himself; that his person is our only asset.

Therefore
We must go to him often, listen to him, do what he says, and act as he does. That's why we are going to follow him during the forty days of his liturgical ascent to his hour.

He is going up to die and then to rise again, to change, to put on the glory of the Son of God. And we are going up with him to learn his ways and change, like him. To reap his harvest, which is eternal Life, that of God the Father.

There are people who will come, start out, and get to the top.
There are others who won't have that much time left.
There are those whose main concern is that nothing should change, but they are getting older just the same.
There are those whose hearts are set only on money, or a new car, or girls, or plenty of drinks every weekend.
There are those who like the prestige but not the work.
The harvest is fine but not the sowing and the tending.
There are those who are busy with . . . what? But they refuse to let it go and pick up the tool.

Consequently, those who come and work will also have to harvest for all these others, for all these friends asleep through ignorance, impervious to the ringing of the alarm. They are like deaf men, and therefore dumb, and the flesh will kill them.

Brothers,

It was for them that you were baptized, that you were led up to this point today. Come on Ash Wednesday too, and on the Wednesdays and Fridays of Lent.

The others—the blind—expect this of you . . . unconsciously.

Your Father and their Father expects this of you; play your parts as elder brothers, as the first called, as wide-awake servants who serve and do not judge.

And may the Lord grant you the grace to *see* these things as he does.

Lent

Before Lent: First Letter

My dear baptized Christians,

single men and women, husbands and wives, parents, public sinners, secret sinners, students, workers, pensioners,

the constant and the fickle,

you who believe in Christ, who pray to him and await his resurrection.

My dear former catechism students, presently members of the Church,

and especially those whom we are awaiting more eagerly because you need more coaxing than the rest,

and you, dear companions in victory and in defeat, the parents of those to whom we longed to give Christ as their treasure,

and you, my dear neighbors, including those who find things to criticize in the way their pastor runs the parish,

and you, dear companions in faith and in toil, who have entrusted the religious education of your children to me for two whole years,

what would this Ash Wednesday, this Lent, this Easter be without you?

It's in order to serve you that the Church calls its members. It counts on them.

May I count on you?

What is a feast day without you? Or the preparations for a feast day without you?

What is a pastor without his parishioners, a frame without a picture, or Christ without a people?

What are ashes, Lent, or Easter without the faithful?

Forget your preconceived notions about your time, about your fellow Catholics, about yourselves, about your neighbors, whether practicing or not, about me, about Christ.

From Ash Wednesday to the Easter Vigil, each Wednesday, Friday, and Sunday will be another precious and necessary stage on the way to a virile and intelligent faith.

Your presence is the first testimony which both believers and unbelievers expect of you.

It's through you that faith falls upon the world like a shower of light or a shower of dust, like a leaven of freedom or a jumble of folklore, like prospects of happiness or shoddy gimcracks at a fair.

Everything here will depend on whether we have worked shoulder to shoulder, or not. Your decision is fraught with consequences which will reflect on us, on God, on yourselves. . . .

If you go ahead, regardless of what people may say, others more timorous than you will follow. Perhaps the Lord will give us a foretaste of his inevitable victory by granting us the unity, the strength, and the joy he has promised to those whom he takes into his service as witnesses.

Before Lent: Second Letter

Whether a child, a student, a trainee, or a *man,* as far as
your Father, your Master, your Instructor, or your *God* is
concerned,
you can equally well be
intimate or stranger,
close or distant,
alike or different.
There is always the same spiritual distance between
the two:
one gives, the other accepts (if he likes)
one speaks, the other listens (if he likes)
one answers, the other asks (if he likes)
one knows, the other will know (if he likes)
one has the capacity, the other the desire (if he likes).
It's similar at school: the teacher supplies the problems,
not the answers.
It's similar at work: the boss supplies the raw materials,
not the finished product.

The same is true with life, the Gospel, the liturgy, the
parables—they all raise problems. So long as you haven't
sweated over them, you are just handling words and empty
ritual. The student must make an effort and find the answer himself if he is to become a scholar, a "wise man."
To find the answer to all this, to life, to liturgy, to the
parables, is to find *peace, charity, justice.*
And that doesn't happen overnight.

Or without effort.
Or without failures.
Or without listening.
Or without trying.

As at school, you can say it's too hard for you, and walk away.

Later you will be very critical of this school which you don't know. You will disparage it in order to vindicate yourself, and make it responsible for every evil.

But the others—mature people—will laugh at you. Among them you will be like an eternal child, fed on assumptions, platitudes, gossip, and magic.

Depending on your environment, you will claim

that faith is ridiculous,

that atheism is ridiculous,

that literature is a waste of time,

that art is kid stuff,

that science turns men into machines,

or . . . just the opposite . . .

Not to know Christ is just as foolish as not to know the basic principles of economics, politics, individual and collective psychology, history. . . .

As a *child,* you know nothing about your environment.

In order to cease being a child, you go to *school,* and you listen to the person who knows. It's not a sin to be a child, but it is a sin not to go to school.

The Church is the Christian's school, and it goes on all his life, all the time of his training. To stop on the way is to ruin his career.

And to make out he's a Christian just the same is to deceive the others, to play-act.

It is to turn into a false witness.

Dear Somebody,

You are one of my former catechism students. But you don't come to church any more.

Are you a turncoat? Or do you think you know all the answers? Or are you waiting for me to call you?

Are you one of those who has stopped going to church, who has forgotten the time of Mass? Are you one of those disciples who, like Judas, lost his taste for Christ?

Or could it be that, like children who believe they are engineers because they "know" that $2 + 2 = 5$, they think their instruction completed because it is begun??? For indeed, they claim the same honors and the same wages as responsible, practicing Christians . . .

I am saying all this because in a few days Lent will start, which leads to Easter.

Make it clear where you stand, either for or against: a genuine atheist is worth more than a fake Christian.

Your new school year starts on Ash Wednesday. We need you.

Before Lent: Third Letter

The Living God calls you to life . . .
in three stages.

He puts you in the *world:*
You like it here. You grow. You experience great pleasures and small troubles.

You are like a child in his parents' house, served by everyone; your wishes are few but they are gratified.

But you grow older, and your troubles grow, for you find your wishes being gratified less and less: you are becoming an adult. And suddenly your joyous childhood appears to you an *unbearable slavery*.

Then he confronts you with *work:*
Instead of being served, you are going to serve.
To join in carrying out his plans.
A chore? No: an adult pleasure.

And what sort of work is it? Serving others? No, building up our world and making it habitable, unifying the human family in the production and peaceful consumption of goods, spirtualizing the land where the Father and Boss wishes to settle with his sons and workers.

So he begins to explain his plans (Word) to you, and his Person.

If you listen, if you get moving, if you fall in with his policy, if you put your heart into *serving* him, he will give you his *Spirit:* his strength, his methods, his health, his genius, his pleasures.

And you willingly trade this everlasting treasure for the pleasures of childhood bondage.

Then, after a span of service, you die and are reborn in heaven, in a life unshackled, in absolute power and absolute light.

So the Living God is calling you.
But in three stages: childhood, training, fruitful maturity.
The pagans call this:
pleasure . . . suffering . . . death.
The philosophers say:
life . . . evil . . . mystery.
Children say:
fun . . . tomorrow . . . nothing.
Some parishioners say:
me . . . the others . . . a disaster.
Jesus will say:
Flesh . . . Follow me . . . Resurrection.
The theologians say:
the Father . . . the Word . . . the Spirit.
The bishops say:
sin . . . penance . . . pardon.
The clergy say:
Christmas . . . Lent . . . Easter.

For hundreds of thousands of years, men have been mulling over this problem. One alone saw: Jesus. And he alone returned to confirm his resurrection in an eternal "Jerusalem."

That's the whole point: Jesus rose and bore witness to it before twelve witnesses, so that they might bear witness to it in their turn from generation to generation. That has been going on now for 2,000 years.

For my part, I believed those witnesses, and have become a witness in my turn, in order to produce new witnesses. I have taken service in Christ's crowd. That is what I was baptized for; that is what baptism effects. Baptism means becoming a witness, or a Christian, officially; it means being publicly accepted as a witness of Jesus' resurrection by Christ, by Christians, by pagans.

In other words, baptism means assignment to the public service.

And *Christian instruction* (which continues all life long) means instruction in the duties of the service.

And *death* is the term of a laborious training, the beginning of a glorious labor.

Like you and me, Jesus experienced these three stages: thirty years of youth, three years of service, then death-resurrection.

You can take Jesus for a fool—if you know him only from gossip.

You can take his witnesses for fakes—if you happen to have met false witnesses, foxes, tigers, ground hogs, asses, and other usurpers of the name of Christian.

You, too, were baptized to serve as a witness to the resurrection and to build up the world of the Risen One.

He cares about you. And he invites you to Lent.

How about it?

Ash Wednesday

> We know that we are dust, and that we
> shall return to dust again.
> BLESSING OF THE ASHES

A prayer for every day of Lent

When fire and wood stay together,
there's light and it's cozy.
When fire and wood fall apart
only ashes remain.
Ashes are dust, dark and formless.
You can't see your way, and everything stops.
So it is with the world and God.

Lord, look
at what we are telling you with these ashes.
We acknowledge, we admit, we proclaim
that we have wrongly driven you away.
You are the fire, the energy, the bread of the world.
Through you the world is able to function.
We want to leave the lowlands of Jericho
and go up with you toward your Jerusalem.
Here we are on the way,
blind and flabby.
During these forty days, be a shepherd to us, Lord,
patiently tending and guiding us.
Gather us around you three times a week
to speak to us and to feed us.

I am ashes,
give me the fire of your life.
Bring me out of the dark dominion of instinct.
Lead me to the dominion of conscience and the Holy
Spirit.

Lent
First Sunday

> Jesus was led into the desert by
> the Spirit, to be tempted by the devil.
> GOSPEL

Three requirements to be brought under control:
requirements of the body, which develop a
    restaurant-religion *(bread);*
requirements of work, which develop a magic-religion
    (giving in to temptation);
requirements of dignity, which develop an atheism-
    religion *(possessing the kingdoms of the earth).*

Three ways of living the Church's life dishonestly:

1. Being a Catholic so as to have a good job, friends, a wife, a husband, an employer, personnel, to be able to provide for all our wants, our daily needs, here summarized under the heading of "bread." That is not what the Church offers. The Church offers the Word and spiritual bread.

2. Being a Catholic because it's useful in business or politics, or in getting a job. For instance, being on good terms with the pastor so as to be able to enlist his aid when we need it.

3. Being a Catholic for self-glorification.

These three temptations—which are really the only ones —are inherent in our nature. We have to eat, we have to enjoy a modicum of success and a certain dignity. But what Satan offers as an ultimate good, Christ declares to be of secondary importance.

You have made your choice: you would rather have eternity than a mess of pottage. But then you must be consistent: follow *your* guide, and don't tie yourself to the other fellow's guides any more.

Lent

Second Sunday

> Tell the vision to no one, till the
> Son of Man has risen from the dead.
> GOSPEL

Christ
calls you to do penance.
He knows why.
Disciple,
put your trust in him.
You'll know why
later on.

God drafts some people,
instructs them,
sends them.
They come,
listen,
and go.

Of his intimates, of you,
Jesus asks still another chore:
to see his *transfiguration*.
Without that, they could
no longer stand fast,
and carry on his job:
to transfigure the world.

Let's explore
the planet Mars with the astronauts,

the Living God with Jesus.
Science and Faith
are two laboratories.
So go explore.

Christ did not come in order to
throw light on problems
which human intelligence can resolve,
but to
light up an approach
to the world of God,
which is beyond our powers.

Faith is not primarily belief
in a system of truths,
but
adherence to a reality.
To believe is to continue Christ's penance
and his radiance.

Lent

Third Sunday

> Arise, O Lord, let not man prevail.
>
> GRADUAL

Arise, O Lord (in me),
don't let instinct have the last word.
May the godless structure of the world
be adapted to your light.
Our routed enemy is already turning tail.
He will stagger and perish under your very eyes.

I am a pitcher
meant for pouring.
If I am filled
with wine,
I shall be useful.
If not . . . what will you do with me?

A devil was making people dumb
(just as in our town).
Jesus casts him out
(through a sacrament).
The dumb man speaks
(as you will, soon).
Because a man who does not speak like God
says nothing.

What is a dumb man?
A man who
will not

receive anything
and *cannot*
give anything:
an empty pitcher.

O pitcher filled with hardened clay,
go, wash,
and the splendor of feasting will be yours again.
Hurry—this is your third Sunday in Lent.

Lent

Fourth Sunday

Whence shall we buy bread that these may eat?
GOSPEL

The multiplication of the "bread" of God in the desert,

or

Moses, manna, the Spirit, and candy

(*see* Numbers 11:10–35)

Act I

1. The people are complaining:
   The desert is all right for five minutes, but
   not for a whole hour,
   especially when you don't understand what it's
   all about and you're longing for all kinds of things—
   except the thing that is urging us into the desert.

2. God gives the nod to the angel of thunderstorms.
   Crash . . . The tents catch fire . . . Howling.

3. Moses, tenderhearted, rushes off to pray for it
   to stop.

4. God agrees.
   Everything gets straightened out. They start off again.
   The spoiled children giggle.

Act II

1. A bunch of semipagans mixed in with the "faithful"
   are grumbling again:
   We're hungry . . . That manna again! More of the
   same lousy stuff!

2. The "faithful" listen to these doltish grumblers,
   and all grumble, whine, complain . . . they rebel . . .
   they want meat, movies, TV, money, etc.

3. They grumble
   as they eat the miraculous manna which instructs
   them (the Word).

4. It breaks Moses' heart to hear people lamenting.
   In his despair at all this, and at all these tears, he asks
   God to kill him rather than force him to educate this
   godless people.
   It's too hard,
   both to become a Christian and to make Christians
   of others . . .
   Moses is a man, like a priest,
   a soft priest, a solitary priest;
   he's fed up too,
   not with serving God but with nagging, with
   hurting (it's inhuman).

5. God is wrathful, he bristles.
   He won't shirk his duty as a Father.
   He has his people brought together.
   (And they all come—that's something, at least.)
   They sanctify themselves (penance).

In the morning, Mass, Communion, sacrifice.
Then, publicly, the 70 best are set apart, and they
receive the Spirit.
Now they are clever and free and strong, just like
Moses.
That's to show what Lent can achieve if it's properly
observed.

Act III

1. The rest get candy, meat, popguns, dolls, drinks,
   girls, money. Everything the world can offer.
   And it's God himself who gives them quail.

2. They scoop up all they can hold. They're delirious
   with joy . . . so happy they could burst.

3. But God sets fire to their guts.
   They lash around in agony . . .
   Mounds of corpses.

4. These princely slaves are buried, slaves of their
   appetite for earthly pleasures.

5. Off they go again, with the survivors.
   They've learned their lesson . . . for a day or two.

Today Jesus recalls this incident
in the history of the Chosen People.
He distributes as much of his coarse rye bread as
the people want.

This time no one grumbles. His deifying Bread:
the Word and the sacraments.
We're in the desert of Lent.
He can give us his Spirit: to all, this time?
Yes? No?
This week,
will you still scorn these gifts of Christ?
Will you insist on earthly candy?
Or will you be one of the 70?
Will you come and pick up the bread of the Wednesdays
and Fridays in our desert?

The Passion

> This is my body which shall be
> given up for you.
> COMMUNION

Challenge:
Only ten days more, and you'll be done with him,
and you'll have your peace; he'll be dead and buried . . .
That's what he wants now, of you:
That's the only means he has left now, with you.
So kill him and smear yourself with his blood.
Then devour him out of malice.

Anything, anything, rather than your indifference.
And in spite of yourself you'll be washed, fed,
instructed by him, God.

Holy Week

Easter is coming.

We all know the shallow type of woman. For her husband, she's a disappointing wife.

She's up to her ears in gossip and household cares, and she treats her husband like one more appliance around the house—an appliance from which she extracts home, money, and children. After which he's put away neatly into a corner, with his paper, his cigarettes, his thoughts, and the TV. She doesn't need his ideas or his friendship. "I'm faithful," she says.

And we all know the *shallow type of Christian*. For Christ, he's a disappointing disciple.

People of this kind treat God as a frame to enhance their dignity. They want him there to help celebrate their birth, their adolescence, their marriage, and, finally, their death. In Russia, they would be atheists; in India, Buddhists; in Africa, Moslems; in Ireland, practicing Catholics; here at home, non-practicing Catholics.

God, for them, is at once a tire patch, glue, varnish, a dustpan, putty, white gloves, and Santa Claus, and his job is to cover up their failures, their coarseness, their deceits and their mysterious hopes—in other words, to guarantee their good opinion of themselves.

These, of course, have always been the gods of the pagans. But what of the Apostles? Did they die for this kind of rubbish?

"Brethren," cries St. Paul, "have this mind in you which was also in Christ Jesus, who though he was by nature God, did not consider being equal to God a thing to be clung to, but emptied himself, taking the nature of a slave and being made like unto men . . . even to death. . . ."

So for the last stage of man's ascent to "salvation," God himself has joined the ranks. For centuries, God was promising men salvation and a Saviour. Now he appoints himself Son of Man. He is in the midst of us today.

What does this mean?

Every man is born a rebel; instinctively he struggles against the tyranny of matter and of his instincts . . . instinctively he plans the supremacy of reason.

The best-known of the leaders of this insurrection (whose history is History) is Jesus of Nazareth.

For instinct, he offers a sublimation in the Spirit (and that Spirit is his). For reason, he offers an infallible tonic (a tonic he possesses). And everything he has, he shares with his comrades in arms, including his divine glory.

Of course, this struggle of humanity for completion is long and bitter. But it's worth it, and liberation is close at hand.

Brother in baptism, if Christmas does not make all this clear to you, then it's no more than a Christmas tree whose dead needles you sweep up in the morning after the midnight festivities. God became man so that you might succeed in becoming God with, through, and in him.

If the shepherds were up and about on Christmas night, it was because they realized that this business concerned them. If, like them, you watch and seek, then come to church: that's where God is born and grows for you. In you.

Christianity must be a mainspring, not a frame in your life. You will make it so only by keeping many a vigil. Wake up then, so that you may awaken others. Come to church, where your fellows keep vigil together in order to awaken together.

But if you still want to sleep the sleep of minerals, vegetables, animals, . . . well, then, sleep well, and may God, your Father, bless your slumbers.

And if you're coming along, then we'll start off, right away, and together, on the ascent to Easter. And then you, too, will make History, which is both sacred and secular.

Easter is coming.

God is in contact with men. He invites them to come to him, in heaven—that everlasting fiesta, free, spiritual. He tells us that heaven is joy of life, the power of living fully and of living together; that the world is the human way of living Life, and heaven the divine way; and that dying means exchanging earth for heaven.

Men have always suspected this, but vaguely and without confirmation; that was the first covenant, the *natural covenant,* cosmic, unconscious.

The first man to take this intuition seriously and to follow it all the way is *Abraham.*

Whereupon God makes an agreement with him, and

Abraham establishes a study center which he will in due course bequeath to his descendants.

This took place 4,000 years ago.

For 2,000 years, God confirms the Jews' ideas, suggests new ones, involves them in field work, transforms their Palestine into a theological laboratory, gives them insights into the future, etc.

Gradually a language all their own develops between God and his earthly study center, a language made up of memories, customs, hopes, rites, symbols—a secret, private language, such as every people invents. This is the *Liturgy*.

Gradually a specialized library grows up, a synthesis of past studies and a tool for current studies. This is the *Bible*.

Gradually certain officials and workers at the Center understand . . . and they offer themselves as guinea pigs, as prototypes, as witnesses. Here we have *Morality*.

Finally it becomes clear that all History, whether Jewish or human, is moving toward the Perfect Man, master of himself, of the world, of heaven, and approved by God. This is Christ, or the *Messias*.

This time, the Center knows that Nature, Liturgy, Bible, and Morals are but four elements in a single process of comprehension of the divine plan, which is that man should entrust to God dominion over the world. So God has not lost time with his Jews. Many people already share his views and are prepared to carry them out.

This was the second covenant, Judaism, or the *Old Testament,* the covenant of the Word.

Now that everything was ready, God sent his only Son as the *Son of Man.*

He was conceived, was born, took his place in the ranks of the Servant-People, in his Father's Center.

When Jesus was thirty years old, God appointed him Director of the Center, and John the Baptist the messianic-king. And John the Baptist hastened to pass this on to the "people on duty."

Then Jesus took over his four elements and worked for three years before the wondering eyes of twelve carefully selected trainees. And when these twelve knew all they had to know about him, he did what still remained to be done but could only be done at the end: *he let himself be sacrificed by his brothers and received by his Father.* His Father made him the risen Man, reborn, glorious, capable of steering his course in God's service.

This was the beginning of the final, perfect covenant, the *New Testament.*

Since the first Pentecost, a God-Man calls upon his disciples to reign with, through, and in him. The new Center is open to all people, and the twelve have turned into thousands of bishops. Through the Word and the Sacraments, they distribute the immense wealth of energy which their leader has laid up in heaven.

The *passage* to God is open to all. And he who comes to know Jesus, easily gives up the old life in exchange for the new. Christians come to the Lord simply and daily to take his orders. As for him, no failure bothers him, no vice disgusts him, no obstacle disturbs him. Through his faithful he calls to the unbelievers and governs all things: the scientific research of the scholars, the religious research of the believers, the constructive labor of the workers, the discipline of his disciples, the atheism of the atheists—he makes use of everything, and everything serves him, as his body once did.

He is central to the world as the head is to the body, as the trunk is to the tree. And his branches bear his fruits. He is central to the people as their king. And his followers are his ministers. He is central to his family as a father. And his sons work as servants who know what their assignment is. For them, heaven has already begun: in them, for them, *through them* . . .

Christians, if you want these words to be filled with light and with joy for you, you know where and how to get instruction and training. No work—no harvest.

Easter is coming. He is, we are risen. Let's
close ranks around him. How about it?
A pastor is nothing; what can I do without
your presence and your work as witnesses?

During Holy Week, Christians celebrate Christ's resurrection.

Palm Sunday

While his enemies, rich and learned, stir up their hatred and plot his death, a few disciples hail him as their king and escort him to the temple.

Holy Thursday

Jesus institutes a *bond* called *communion* and personally offers it to each disciple present. He will thus be able to draw them to himself after his leap into death, which will carry him to God in a few hours.

Good Friday

Of his own will, Jesus makes the leap, dies, leaves our shores. He lets himself be killed for God and offered to God like the lamb sacrificed each year at the Jewish Passover, like Isaac bound to the fagots on the great stone before the ritual slaying and burning.

Holy Saturday

Jesus is dead. Drowned in the ocean of death, in which all men end their forty- or eighty-years' struggle for life. All that remains are some words, some promises, an example, . . . and a small group of terrified believers, bewildered at his failure, but who still believe what he said of himself: *I am God.*

Easter Vigil: light—water—bread

These three striking symbols sum up Jesus' thoughts on time, life, men, and the creative power which the sacraments confer on men.

Easter Sunday

Jesus rises, issues forth from death, becomes the first man, the New Adam of a new earth, on the other shore of life— heaven. With him, the human race reaches fulfillment. His heroic faith and obedience make of him the first sheaf in the human harvest to be gathered in the sacred barns. Through him, the long history of man stops being absurd. The Word was made flesh in order to be the first *holy* man received by God in God.

Easter

> Christ, our Passover, has been
> sacrificed.
> EPISTLE

Response of the dead
to the dead man who eludes them by rising.

Response of the dead
to the living man who raises their archetype of death.

Response of Christians
to God, their Father.

It's only by being *truthful*
about the liturgy, the Bible, morals, mysticism,
that a priest and his parish discover
that they were practicing, honoring, perpetuating
a *falsehood*.

That they were debasing their Christianity
into a humanistic, legalistic, formalistic screen
for the cowardice of the Peters, for the coarseness of
the Judases.

Falsehood is cruel to truth . . . Jesus dies of it.
Truth is cruel to falsehood . . . Jesus, now become sin for us, dies.
Truth, in Jesus, kills Peter and Judas.

But the death, in Jesus, of the old man
opens, in him, the career of the new humanity,
the spiritual career of his disciples.

Peter and Judas harbored the man of yesterday.
Jesus, risen, harbors the man of tomorrow.
He makes the old model obsolete.
He introduces the new man.

Thanks be to him who saves us
from the dead end of the earth,
and opens up heaven to us.
Thank you on behalf of all the Peters and Judases,
Thank you!

"Christ has risen from the dead,
by death trampling upon death,
and has bestowed life
upon those in the tombs."

> (Verse chanted twenty-five times by the people during the Easter Vigil in the Greek Church.)

The focal point of the Faith
is this good news:
the coming and the Lordship of Jesus
through his resurrection.

Let's get moving, so that he may draw us
into his team, into his eternal people.

Jesus the Ferryman has made his Easter duty.
If you're getting into his boat
it's to make your Easter duty too:
to "pass over" with him.

Easter = pass over,
through death,
from the life of earth to the life of heaven,
from the earthly state to the divine.

Easter

First Sunday

> Beloved, all that is born of God
> overcomes the world; and this is the victory
> that overcomes the world, our faith.
> EPISTLE

Pentecost = Harvest

O you who are risen,
let us eat of the tree of life.
Let us sing the wonders of God.
Let us enjoy the promised land.
After forty days of Lent come fifty days of glory.
From Easter to Pentecost we celebrate
the springtime of the New Creation.

In heaven, three bear witness:
the Father, the Son, and the Spirit;
and these three are but one.

On earth, three things bear witness,
three sacramental signs:
the Spirit of Confirmation,
the water of Baptism,
and the Blood of the Eucharist.

Easter

Second Sunday

> For you were as sheep going astray, but
> now you have returned to the shepherd and
> guardian of your souls.

EPISTLE

The word of God:

"Woe to the shepherds who mislead and scatter the
flock of my pasture . . .
You have scattered my sheep and driven them away.
You have not cared for them,
but I will take care to punish your evil deeds.
I myself will gather the remnant of my flock . . . they
shall increase and multiply.
I will appoint shepherds for them who will shepherd them
so that they need no longer fear and tremble, and none
shall be missing . . .
I will raise up a righteous shoot to David; as king
he shall reign and govern wisely . . ."
 Then my people will live in security, prosperity, and
  peace.
And this shepherd will be God-with-Everyone, God who
solves all problems.

(Jeremia)

Woe to the shepherds who feed themselves and sacrifice
the flock for their own comfort. They have not strengthened the sick sheep, tended the wounded ones, cared for

93

the mothers, carried the lambs, brought back the strays, looked for the lost.

You have led them harshly and brutally. And they are at the mercy of all the wild beasts (untrained instincts). I shall save my lambs, I shall tear them from your mouths. I shall come myself among my sheep. I shall inspect them. I shall lead them to shelter in good pastures. I myself will pasture them and give them peace. I shall look after the weaklings and the sick.

As for you, my lambs, I shall sort you out too; I shall remove the rams and the he-goats and the fat sheep that eat the share of the lean ones and butt the weak out of the way. I shall give them a good shepherd who will do his work well, a David, a faithful servant. Then I shall make a final peace convenant with him that will put an end to all opposition. There will be neither yoke nor suffering any more.

(Ezechiel)

"The Lord is my shepherd; I shall not want.

In verdant pastures he gives me repose; beside restful waters he leads me; he refreshes my soul. He guides me in right paths for his name's sake.

Even though I walk in the dark valley, I fear no evil; for you are at my side with your rod and your staff that give me courage.

You spread the table before me in the sight of my foes; you anoint my head with oil; my cup overflows. Only goodness and kindness follow me all the days of my life; and I shall dwell in the house of the Lord for years to come."

(Psalm 22)

Easter
Third Sunday

> Let those who profess to be Christians
> avoid whatever will endanger their faith,
> and follow those things which will help it.
> COLLECT

Yesterday, Jesus,
the Man of God,
was the living message of God,
the face that he turned toward twelve disciples.
Today, the Church,
the People of God,
is the living message of God,
the face he turns
toward three billion atheists.

There is only one testimony on behalf of God:
the risen Jesus.
There is only one testimony that supports Jesus:
the historical adventure of the Jewish people.
There is only one testimony in support of the risen Jesus:
the historical unity of the Christian people.

A Christian is a sign:
a living sign of God,
a living sign of what God is, wants, is able to effect,
a sign of the wisdom of God.
Every Christian
is a trail blazer

who clears a new path
for his spiritual younger brothers.

Every Christian
is a Christ
at any given time and place.

The pastor gives
verbal witness
in the Church.
The layman gives
witness of holy living
in the market place.
The one is useless without the other.

Easter

Fourth Sunday

> That their hearts may always be
> fixed upon the true happiness of heaven.
> COLLECT

Meeting Christ personally,
working under his orders at "finishing" the world,
is only a stage in a process.
Possessing his Spirit,
his breath, and his joy—
that is completion.

When the city dweller comes to the country,
he looks at the farmer and exclaims:
"What a wonderful life!"
And he makes straight for an agricultural school.
And he is perfectly right.

When he has found a farm to take over,
he sets to work with enthusiasm and says:
"What a hard life!"
And he's right; it's a hard life but a
good one.

Religion isn't what we dream it to be either;
It's harder and much more beautiful.

Ascension

May our minds dwell always
on this heavenly home.
COLLECT

Man's growth
is an ascension
beyond the world
up to divinity.
A tough climb. A joyous victory.

The Ascension
is an image
carved out of Christ's flesh;
it comes after deep purification
in order to speak to you about yourself.

Ascension
through death:
that is the point. . . .
And, if you wish,
this way lies open to you in the Church.

The future
is a world under God's governance, says the Bible;
it is Man-in-God, says Christ;
I am the future, says Jesus, the One who is Risen.

The past
is the obsolete, the devil, the tempter;

it is a retreat, a repetition, the easy way, the least;
it is the known, the rigid, the backward looking.

Choose.

The "flesh"
or "world"
is the tyrannical law of matter.
The "Spirit"
or "grace"
is the law which masters matter.

You must choose, as Christ did.

Sunday After the Ascension

. . . make our wills devoted to you so that our hearts
may sincerely serve your majesty.

COLLECT

Introit

"Hear, O Lord, my voice as I cry to you, Alleluia! My heart
has spoken to you; I have sought you. Your presence, O
Lord, I will seek; hide not your face from me, Alleluia,
Alleluia!

The Lord is my light and my salvation, whom should I
fear?"

Epistle (I Peter 4:7–11)

"Beloved: Be prudent and watchful in prayers. But
above all things have a constant mutual charity among
yourselves; for charity covers a multitude of sins. Be hos-
pitable to one another without murmuring. According to
the gift that each has received, administer it to one another as good stewards of the manifold grace of God.

If anyone speaks, let it be as with words of God. If anyone ministers, let it be as from the strength that God fur-
nishes; that in all things God may be honored through
Jesus Christ our Lord."

Alleluia

"God reigns over all the nations, God sits on his holy throne, Alleluia!

I will not leave you orphans; I go away, but I will come to you, and your heart shall rejoice. Alleluia!"

Gospel (John 15:26–27; 16:1–4)

After the Last Supper, Jesus said to his disciples: "When the Advocate has come, whom I will send you from the Father, the Spirit of truth who proceeds from the Father, he will bear witness concerning me. And you also will bear witness, because from the beginning you are with me. These things I have spoken to you that you may not be scandalized. They will expel you from the synagogues. Yes, the hour is coming for everyone who kills you to think that he is offering worship to God. And these things they will do because they have not known the Father nor me. But these things I have spoken to you, that when the time for them has come you may remember that I told you."

Offertory

"God ascends his throne amid shouts of joy, the Lord is taken up with the sound of trumpets, Alleluia!"

Communion

"Father, while I was with them, I kept them whom you gave me, Alleluia! but now I am coming to you; I do not pray that you take them out of the world but that you keep them from evil, Alleluia, Alleluia!"

Pentecost

Pentecost

> Come, Holy Spirit, fill the hearts of your faithful,
> and kindle in them the fire of your love.
>
> GRADUAL

Together
we await what the Lord promised:
Pentecost.

Christmastide
concerned the *hope* of men
torn by the contradictions of the world.

Paschaltide
reflected on the work of a man
victorious over all these contradictions, even over death.
It was Jesus, son of Mary and of God, who was
that first total man who triumphed by virtue of the Spirit.

The season of Pentecost
will show us how the victory of one
becomes the victory of all.

Fire
is an enthralling power
clearly bespeaking joy, strength, independence.

It's easy to see why fire should be associated, as a symbol, with celebrations in the country, in the city, and in the Church.

There's fire in a look, in a voice, in a character.

So it's natural to use fire as a symbol for the Spirit of God. That Spirit *caught in Jesus.*

It made of Jesus the first sheaf in that harvest of free men which God expects of an earth made new in him.

We shall soon be celebrating this *harvest* in a special way, in connection with those children who are completing their catechism course. Are they to be regarded as privileged persons or as victims?

First Communion
is not just *their* celebration but that of all those in our parish who sow the Words of God in our village so that one day our people may reap the Spirit.

We know from Christ that others come in the night: enemies who sow nettles, lies.

But he said that this didn't matter, and didn't concern us for the time being.

The children of our catechism class, then, will become sowers of truth or falsehood, of the good Word or of weeds, according to whether their elders stand by them or corrupt them. Stand by them, or ignore them, or lead them astray.

In ten years' time, their elders will have turned them into the kind of persons who are straightforward or untruthful, alive or dull, active or fearful, awake or somnolent, instructed or ignorant, leaders or cavilers, hypocrites or unassuming.

These elders are in the first place those who are closest to the children: father, mother, brothers, relatives, neighbors, parishioners.
Let them keep this responsibility in mind.

If their religion has no practical expression, if it is without light and strength of renewal, without effect on their interior, exterior, or social life, then they are condemning innocent souls to indifference, betrayal, and the absurdity of a folk religion.

One doesn't trifle with love, least of all with the love of God.

The Patriarch of Moscow recently excommunicated a bishop merely because he had shown himself a little timorous in the face of official hostility. This elderly man knows how to choose between God and man, between the Spirit and the world . . .

Do we?

Trinity Sunday

> Make lasting what you have wrought in us,
> O God!
>
> OFFERTORY OF PENTECOST

Today is the first Sunday after Pentecost,
the first day of Christian school.

Medicine has a long history;
it begins with herbs
and goes all the way to antibiotics.

Architecture has a long history;
it begins with caves
and goes all the way to skyscrapers.

Transportation has a long history;
it begins in the branches
and goes right out into the cosmos.

Hunting, too, covers a lot of ground;
it begins in the forests
and continues in the supermarkets.

Religion has a long history;
it begins with Adam and Eve,
it is summed up in Mary and Jesus Christ.

Each branch of human endeavor began by growing a
slender shoot, then groped its way, faced opposition, en-
dured the trials of time.

In each branch, the men most gifted for the work concerned have specialized, struggled for the common victory, defied public inertia and the dangers of failure, contempt, and ostracism.

For hundreds of thousands of years, these bold seers have been opening up the roads of our future, stationed at the tips of their respective branches, and have done their part to give humanity its legitimate place under the sun, its sound trunk, its fruits, its security, its peace.

For hundreds of thousands of years, man has been doing on-the-job training in how to administer the universe.

Not many biologists, physicists, engineers, politicians, sociologists, and artists blaze a trail into the future.

But the few who do are followed. And if they are proved right, then their following increases, and one fine day everyone thinks and does the same. . . .

Religion is one of these branches of human endeavor that strives for the noontide of its destiny and the full deployment of its energies.

Christ's school has few enough students, even though many people bear his name and put a cross over the mantel or around their necks.

The local school has many pupils. But how many are scholars? To be a disciple involves discipline. And to discipline oneself requires time, determination, and discrimination.

Christians are Christ's school. Some of them are his disciples. They are few, despised, regarded by most people as useless, vain, and insincere. Why?

Because those who take their Christian schooling seriously are hampered by the others in their work and in their witness. They are swamped in a sea of pseudo Christians. Some of these have not set foot inside the school since they were twelve years old. Others develop their own brand of Christianity, which they use for various purposes as a financial, cultural, political, literary, or sentimental tool. And there are those glib talkers who think they are Christians, and call themselves Christians.

Lots of young students have thought they were "existentialists" because of reading a book.

Lots of painters have thought of themselves as surrealists because they have done poor imitations of a great painter.

Lots of boys have thought of themselves as leaders because they have stuck three feathers in their caps, or thrown firecrackers on the pavement, or got a girl in trouble, or caused suffering to a neighbor.

My fellow Christian,

today, Christ's school is open to you.

Come in.

Pentecost
Fourth Sunday

> Henceforth thou shalt catch men.
> GOSPEL

And now, Callista, since you have read and
understood the Gospel, you'll understand the Epistle too.
You'll see what St. Paul calls water,
what he calls the ship's regulations,
what he calls the lifeboat,
the name he gives to the gentleman who appears to be
asleep.

And you'll accept the strict discipline of your life
in the crew, in the Church.
You'll accept the diet, duties, schedules, chores, and
patience of a sailor's life.

Pentecost

Seventh Sunday

> Do men gather grapes from thorns, or figs from
> thistles?
> GOSPEL

Our job, our mission, is to tell about Christ.
But you can only tell of what you've heard.

As you choose your food, so you will bear fruit.
Don't sell your goods as something they're not,
or without knowing that they're something different.
The others will not be deceived.

The Christian thrives on work.
Before he found Faith, all his effort was directed to
possessing it.
After finding Faith, his job is now to give it.
Absence from work means absence from the payroll.

On the outside: a face, features, words, gestures,
a body. On the inside: a character, mind, ideas, soul,
faith.
The inside is what counts.
The outside is what talks.

Don't talk about what doesn't count for you,
about what you're not.
Proclaim your faith, Christ.

Pentecost
Tenth Sunday

> Two men went up to the temple to pray, the one
> a Pharisee and the other a publican . . .
> GOSPEL

God will reveal
the pettiness of the braggart,
the greatness of the lowly.

He will bring down
the man who exalts himself.

He will exalt
the man who acts humbly.

Pentecost

Eleventh Sunday

> "Ephepheta," that is, "Be thou opened."
> GOSPEL

Laws for humanizing the flesh:
1. To strain toward Christ with our feet.
2. To strain toward Christ with our ears.
3. To strain toward Christ with our mouths.

The order of these three stresses has to be observed in every kind of education—academic, liturgical, moral, political, and economic.

I have announced good news to you.
Now I am going to explain it more and more.

For your part, you have agreed.
Now you are setting off along this road,
and you will be counted among the blessed.

But if you don't do what I say,
then your faith is meaningless.

The stages of faith:
1. To love God.
2. To try to hear him.
3. To carry out his plans.

112

Practical application:
Joyfully baptize anyone wandering between the first and second stages who asks for baptism.
Refuse baptism to anyone who has not yet reached the first stage.

God is a father.
And you, what are you before him?
a child?
an adult?

Every disobedient child is an atheist in the bud.
Every obedient child is a believer in the bud.

The disobedient adolescent is an atheist who is not yet ripe.
The obedient adolescent is a Christian who is not yet ripe.

The disobedient adult is indifferent.
The obedient adult is a mature man.

I am talking of obedience to God.

A *word* of the Scriptures
is no more than a seed.

That seed must ripen
through commentaries in church.

And the flowers must turn into fruit
through your actions in the town.

Pentecost

Twelfth Sunday

> And who is my neighbor?
>
> GOSPEL

Let's look and listen.
Jesus is explaining himself and explaining things to us.
The parable of the *good* Samaritan.

The night. That's what he thinks of the present time. But he is there because the night is far advanced. Day is dawning. We must be ready to celebrate noon, the eternal *noon*.

With him, we must generate that noontide of humanity's radiant maturity.

The way. Man's life stretches between two poles: nothingness and total reality (God).

Jericho, symbol of nothingness, is the alluring city of the world as such; Jerusalem symbolizes the city of man with the ideas and laws of God.

The inn symbolizes the city of man with God in person: the New Jerusalem, the Church.

Oil and wine: symbols of the Word and the sacraments which Jesus, God, bears, brings with him, places within our reach.

The beast of burden symbolizes the gift he makes to us of his own means of succeeding in the human adventure of scaling the heaven of the Father of the world.

The robbers symbolize everything we have already experienced in life when force alone is right. When the law of the jungle prevails, we are all robbers and robbed, brutes and victims of brutality.

Priests and Levites: symbols of the better men who know God's ideas, yet who parade past selfishly, quite pleased with themselves if they pray and do "very little." They shirk the *essential* gesture, the one which creates the future world of man with God: to love one's neighbor as one's self.

The Samaritan. The word means "keeper." For the Jew, the Samaritan was a stranger, despised, rejected by all: Jesus. But he, God, having the right Spirit, goes up to the man who is in pain and stuck on the road, he sets him on his own beast, and pays all the expenses for as long as necessary. The man who is strong goes out to the other; where there is no humility, there is no real contact.

Jericho: the moon.
The beast of burden: the flesh of Christ.
The inn: the Church.
The morrow: the resurrection.
Two silver pieces: the two approaches of the two testaments.

A question: "Who is my neighbor?"
A strange answer: "It's up to you to act like a neighbor."

An explanation:
a rescuer must draw near;

the rescued must simply accept.
Everyone, including Jesus, is by turn
rescuer and rescued, eater and eaten.
That is the dialogue of genuine love.

We all dream of having friends eager to do things for us . . .

But that means that each of us must fulfill the dream of every other man, known or not, pleasant or not, rich or not.

Why? Because humanity is an entity, created to be united in a single Spirit, God's, to accomplish a single task, Christ's.

Today's Mass is neither more nor less than this miracle in process of realization. In the Mass, God comes to meet his creatures and delivers to them his secrets, his person, his eternal and triumphant universe.
He explains them to the world and the only intelligent use of the world, which is
to create unity.

We all need each other's heart, hands, and faculties.

Pentecost
Thirteenth Sunday

> And as he was entering a certain village,
> there met him ten lepers.
>
> GOSPEL

The *Law*—this word covers all the work God expects
of Man (Adam) in the world.
What is that work? To build a world in which God will
be willing to live with us (six days).
A covenant with the Jewish people (Old Testament) spells
out that work.
Man created (appointed) by God is to administer the world
and bring it to the eternal Sunday of total prosperity.
God expects of his servants the fruit of his land and the
product of their labors.

But God is not a master in the manner of human masters.
He doesn't let his servant finish a hard job alone; he does
the hardest part himself.
He doesn't eat the fruits of the work alone or before the
workers. He doesn't relegate them to the kitchen.
In becoming flesh, he comes right down into the factory.
Through his sacrifice, he provides food and drink.
By "speaking," he becomes host, home, light . . .
He is all that every mother is for her child,
every father for his son.
Better still: even before the work is done (for the past 2,000

years), he rings the bell that announces the banquet (Communion).

That's how Jesus explains himself.

But he backs up the incredible news of this invitation with an object lesson, a real-life parable: the healing of the ten lepers.

A number of biblical themes intersect at this point.

The leprosy theme. The leper is banished from the village. Only the priests, after numerous examinations, waiting periods, and sacrifices, have authority to restore him to the community of the healthy. An excellent image of heresy and its consequences.

The Jerusalem theme. There is the temporary city and the other, the body of Christ, the Kingdom—longed for, begun, but completed only in Christ and through him.

Theme of the Law, of the way, of the crossroads, of the caravans: that of Christ and his followers—all those who seek after God—advancing to meet a hostile world.

Theme of the king who heals, of the shepherd who gathers his flock.

Theme of sin as leprosy, healed by the personal touch of God immediately upon an appeal for help, as soon as there was a beginning of submission (penance). But the priest alone has authority to define the legal consequences of the cure and the return to society. (Here we recognize the rhythm and the true dimensions of confession: God's part in it, the priest's, and that of the triumphant survivor who comes to show that he himself has been made clean, and requests certification of his fitness to return to the royal clan.)

Theme of the choice, the selection, in which each Christian is personally involved.

Themes of the five movements, or stages, of the flesh to the Spirit, of the night to glory, which the liturgy analyzes every day before our eyes:

1. the movement toward God at the prompting of the individual conscience: *Introit;*
2. the movement toward Christ (listening to readings, hymns, sermon): *word;*
3. the movement toward the altar for the *offering* of one's self to the master of the work;
4. the movement in Christ for the banquet of *Communion;*
5. the movement in Christ to summon towns and villages, fields and factories, pagans, atheists and leprous heretics, a joyous streaming of the liberating army: *Ite, missa est,* mission.

Theme of the Law which defines sin but does not heal it.

Pentecost

Fourteenth Sunday

How lovely is your dwelling place, O Lord!
INTROIT

What is the Earth?
a garden?
a school?
an office?
a workshop?
a drawing room?
a cradle?
a bar?
a prison?
a stage?
a prize ring?
a dungeon?
a torture chamber?
a cemetery?
a mother's womb?
a father's estate?

Lord and dear God, the world
is the workshop
of the Kingdom of *you and us.*
Work has become a joy
since we know that,
and since your only Son
has been working among us and with us.
He talks as he works,

he explains things,
and we know that all is well,
and anxiety and sloppy workmanship disappear.

Those who want to understand this Mass of the Fourteenth Sunday after Pentecost will read Chapters 52 and 53 of Isaia.

But watch out!
It's written for very plain men,
not for the clever—
For people who have died to their instincts
and risen with Jesus—
For people who trust in God.

Pentecost

Fifteenth Sunday

> At that time, Jesus went to a town called Naim.
> GOSPEL

Two processions are coming . . . and going. . . .
One comes from Jerusalem (heaven) and goes toward Jerusalem (heaven) with its growing harvest of the risen.
The other comes from Naim (the world) with its dead man (a harvest that has failed, defective goods) toward a cemetery (nothingness), before returning to Naim where only the (spiritually) dead are born, fit for the cemetery.
The procession of the Son of God is a kind of river of Life, of health, of joy.
The procession of the son of man, of Eve, of humanity without God, weeps over its hopeless misery.
These two peoples bear their two heroes like two banners: Life here, death there.
Two destinies: the old and the new.
One is saved through faith in Jesus; the other lost in
the consequences of sin.
One has met the envoy of salvation. The other does not know him yet and plods on.

Meeting.
Will the crowd and the widow carrying her offspring notice who is passing? Will they stop, ask, let themselves be moved, believe?
They stop in their progress toward the absurd. In tears,

they offer themselves to the Saviour (humble confession both of their helplessness and of his power). And that is enough.

Jesus stops too. They had sensed his call. He will "say" (do) what he is, what he has, what he has the power to do. He "touches" (sacramental contact). He speaks: "Arise!"

And the dead man, vivified by the body of Christ, arises with an active faith which sings the glory of God; he "believes" what Jesus says. He has come into the Church, the new people of men, the sons of the New Adam.

Every Sunday, Christ and his own pass through the community. Some waylay him and follow him and let themselves be grafted on this tree of life.

Others pass by, throw their dead anywhere but to him, and believe only in the meager powers of Naim. . . . They remain true to this lifeless mother, to this wedding feast where the wine has failed, to this flesh without Spirit, to this woman without a husband, to this creation without a creator, to this world without God, to this lamp without oil, to this death without resurrection, to a godless life.

Every Sunday, the crossroads of fortune emerge out of the mist, and those who weep and stop and wait . . . see him and come to life again.

The incident reflects Christ's judgment on the world, on history, liberty, suffering. It is a systematic analysis of them.

Those who do not stop at Christ go off to gods who are

easier to understand and follow, and quick to pay their miserable wages. Crushed between their helplessness and the law, they choose to go no further.

But the Church is the crossroads of the Flesh and the Spirit. There the two streams converge.

Pentecost
Sixteenth Sunday

> At that time, when Jesus entered the house of
> one of the rulers of the Pharisees on the Sabbath
> to take food, they watched him.
> GOSPEL

How shall we build the unity of the world? How shall we
gather around God's table, which is the world, *all* God's
guests, all the sons of God, the whole human family of
God?
How can we reconcile all these rival, contradictory an-
archical trends?
Breaking in a car means adjusting each of its parts:
slowly,
tactfully,
with discretion,
with prudence,
with restraint.
Each part must keep its own shape but lose its roughness,
its unevenness, its sharp corners.
You can't keep a part which insists on remaining rigid,
unadaptable, unchangeable. It would break the others and
become completely useless itself . . .

The Sadducees? They must change this . . .
The Pharisees? They must change that . . .
The mass of ordinary people? They must change . . .

The intellectuals who talk and don't act . . .

The manual workers who listen and believe the garrulous or the strong, instead of thinking for themselves . . .

The atheists . . .
The Catholics . . .

The conservatives . . .
The liberals . . .

The young . . .
The older people . . .

The practicing Catholics who proclaim and perform half of their duties—the spectacular half . . .
The non-practicing Catholics who proclaim and perform the other half—the invisible half . . .

No car comes out of the plant all broken in and ready for the road.

No man emerges complete from his mother, his baptism, his studies, his bed.

When everyone has been "broken in," life together will be wonderful.

Those who don't want to complete *themselves* . . . that's exactly what is not your business, since you can't yet claim to be complete yourself; take your place, take the whole of it, but only yours.

Pentecost

Eighteenth Sunday

> Arise, take up thy pallet and go to
> thy house.
>
> GOSPEL

Today's Mass develops its message on three levels: the historical, the liturgical, and the moral.

1. Historical. Recalling the past, from Jesus back to Abraham.
2. Liturgical. The same realities are actualized through "signs" for the congregation of believers.
3. Moral. Directed to the world at large, showing paralytics standing up and vivified by their contact with Jesus: the people of the Holy Spirit.

Jesus' movements are deliberate. He comes down from the mountain (from God). He crosses the lake (from his world to ours). He lets those with faith in his power bring him their sick. He heals the paralytic (consequence of sin, sign of sin). He returns him to his own people to serve both as living evidence and as a witness (meaning of the *Ite, missa est*).

Then, in this solemn setting, come his blunt commentaries, anticipated by each member of the cast:

I heal sin. . . . I come and I redeem the mortgage of evil and death.

I come as a son of man, yet I heal in my own name.

I come because you are as you are, and to give you what you hope to be.

You know that one must come who was promised: the Messias, the Christ, the accomplished Son of Man, the King of the world and of men. I am he.

I, God, am come to fulfill an agreement; I prove myself by showing myself. Watch everything I do—my gestures, my words.

Remember all that our prophets foretold concerning me, including Daniel in his Chapter 7, particularly from verse 9 on.

Let's read that text over again.

Now we understand the two reactions of the Jews around him:

For the scribes: he claims to be God (healing); he blasphemes; he must be put to death.

For the crowd: he has divine powers; he is the Messias; in him God is present (awe).

The enthusiasm which sweeps the crowd is that of people who obscurely perceive that they are experiencing a historic moment. Some wind of universal victory is blowing there, of a sharing of the spoils, of a miraculous haul of fish, of an earthly paradise—supra-earthly.

The world's boss is taking charge.

The guerrillas feel assured of supplies, arms, and leadership. . . . Faith in Jesus has brought them into the final Noah's Ark, into the caravan of the ultimate Moses, into the Kingdom of the perfect David.

Men have always puzzled over the mystery of the world. For 4,000 years, that of the Jewish message; for 2,000 years, that of Jesus and his people. Since last night, that of this morning's Mass (for the believers have been praying, fasting, studying since yesterday so as not to be late for today's appointment). Half an hour ago, they left their homes to go to meet him who comes to save the paralytics that are brought to him.

So they bring themselves, and they will be touched (Word and bread). They will leave restored, to show themselves, to bear witness to the good news before the world.

The Epistle describes their new attitude, their mission as healed patients singing the glories of their healer. They have gathered beyond the lake (nothingness), where Jesus is, and their baptism and their Church (people).

And here they are, welded into a spiritual height where they are safe from the nothingness into which the weight of time drags down the flesh.

Pentecost
Nineteenth Sunday

> So that both in body and soul we may be
> eager to do your will.
> COLLECT

Let us read the *Introit* to the Mass; let us sing it slowly, joyfully, to ourselves.

Then let us step into the train, into the caravan that is starting up, pulling away, getting up speed: the *Epistle*.
Justice? a new interior condition, a new domestic policy.
Holiness? a new external policy, of adherence to God, the Lord.
Servicing by Christ, the mechanic, the craftsman, the brilliant, sensitive, vigorous artist who comes to complete what he began, to save what he created, to harvest what he sowed; who becomes "us" by a marriage bond, as the prophets foretold.

Mutation in the depths of the spirit.

Gradual. Alleluia: let us hold fast to our friendly relations with the Boss.

In the *Gospel,* Jesus speaks to the professionals, to those who really know their Bible. All they need is the prick of the lancet to open the abscess—if they want it opened . . .

The King? Yahweh: the immeasurable God.

The Son? Jesus: that little man . . . the divine Prince, the heir, the ambassador, the Messias. He comes to seek the *Bride* whom his Father has made for him.

The Betrothed? Jerusalem, all humanity.

After the nuptial bath (the age-old baptism begun in Moses and culminating in Jesus), he invites the guests to form a procession (the Church) to go up to his father's house, where the table is spread for the banquet of the gods: the dazzling hall of the eternal wedding feast.

As is customary, friends (prophets) have been sent. The preliminaries have been completed. The sacrificial lamb is ready, that food which men and God can eat together without being destroyed by it, for both produced it: the Son of God and men together.

The *animal?* obtained from the divine farm (the world) administered by the servant Adam, his race, his descendant . . .

And behold the bridegroom, ours, the one who will fructify human endeavor for always. His love is so ardent that he comes himself to seek out the reticent bride: his people, his friends, his children, his future guests and fellow workers. In him, the Creator awaits the completed Creature . . .

He struggles, explains, shows himself, opens himself to them, explains their own fears to them, clears the way for them, heals, straightens, feeds, answers, asks . . .

As with parents who try to bring their baby out of babyhood: anger and kisses alternate continuously till they have succeeded in turning the baby into a child, an adolescent, an adult, a friend, a partner.

Such is Jesus in this parable.
The simple of heart will follow him. The others won't.

Pentecost

Twentieth Sunday

> At that time, there was a certain royal official
> whose son was lying sick at Capharnaum. When
> he heard that Jesus had come from Judea into
> Galilee, he went to him.
>
> GOSPEL

At Cana, we have the mystery of water, baptism,
rebirth.
In Christ, the Word made flesh, the child Adam achieves
the maturity of the adult. The trainee becomes a full-
fledged worker.
Adam dies, the Son of God appears: he appears as a Son of
Man.
He who sought to usurp God's throne is to receive Divinity.
Death and resurrection. The caterpillar turns into a
butterfly.
The flesh finally emerges from chaos, nothingness, night,
sin, time.

At Cana, where he changed water into good and plentiful
wine, he changed sickness into health.
Instead of the earthly wine stolen by Adam, he gives the
wine of heaven.
Wine is for joy—the joy of life, health, laughter, under-
standing.

Earthly wine counterfeits and stupefies. Christ's wine (Communion) makes you godlike, clever, resourceful, powerful, rich.

Earthly wine makes you sick. That of the sacraments gives life.

Here, confronting one another, are the true and false divinities.

Who is this, standing before Jesus? An official of King Herod, the fundamental adversary, the absolute opponent. Here is the man who is his right hand, his eye, his ear, his officer, his collaborator, his little pal in his orgies and murders. Here is Herod. Here is the murderer, the deicide, the God-killer, the absolute idiot, the rival, the counter-king, the man responsible for the rebellion in Eden: Adam, the usurper. Here is the false king, the false prophet, the false priest, the false god, the prototype of the sinner.

And here is Jesus, the true possessor of all those titles which Herod has usurped. What are we going to see? . . . Man is going to pay with his tears for many thousand years of obscenities, betrayals, thefts, lies. They will shout what they think of each other. The ultimate battle will be fought out in public, clear-cut and decisive. We shall know where we stand. They will deliver the world from the dark secret which oppresses and stultifies it. All power to the victor!

Herod: "My son, fruit and product of my world, myself . . . is sick to death. You are Life. You are the Living One. I am the dead man.

"You are strong, you are all. I'm not. Yesterday I was lying. I was robbing your name and your garments. I am Cain, Jacob, Babylon, Moloch, the usurper, ridiculous and defeated.

"God is you . . . not I. I declare it. I acknowledge it.

"It is you who create me. Not I who create, invent, manufacture, construct you.

"You are the doctor, I the sick man. You are wise, I am mad. You are right, I am wrong.

"You are the master, I the servant. You are the Creator, I the creature.

"Do your job so that I may continue to do mine well: make me, finish me. I can't do it. Make a pact with me. Here is my person. Give me yours. Here I am. Give me yourself. Hand yourself over.

"I understand now. Be the Father again, as when I was little, innocent, in the cradle of the earthly paradise."

And Jesus, without batting an eyelid, saves Herod, saves the monster, saves all the Herods, for there are only Herods on earth. He gives him his life, his glory, his titles, his name . . . Because he asks.

And so Herod *communicates:* Herod (in his officer, and the officer in his son) recovers health, life, world, joy, glory, work: the mission to serve the true King, God his Father.

The first Mass of Herod-Adam is over. He returns home to celebrate his own feast.

Yesterday that man was an officer of the clown-king, a subject of the clown-king; now he is an officer of Christ, the eternal and generous King, a member of Christ, King and God.

And that man is you . . .

Pentecost
Twenty-second Sunday

> Render, therefore, to God the
> things that are God's.
> GOSPEL

His enemies thought they could trap him
by playing politics,
but he raises the debate to a different level.

Of course there is a Caesar!
But Caesar is only Adam, man, any man, all men whose
job it is to construct and govern this world.
Does he have the power, the talents, he needs for this job?

Caesar is
science, technology, the arts,
ready to hand.
Whether he is a Jew or a Roman, he's fine so
long as he keeps to his proper place.

Caesar is a good skipper,
but he's under the orders of the Admiral,
who is God, your Father.
It is God who provides the boat and the wind
and the sea and the supplies and the home port
and the chart and the destination.
And there, you'll get your promotion,

the promotion of an only son, a cherished son,
who has proved himself a good and faithful servant.

Science and its techniques,
faith and its morals,
are the two eyes and the two hands
of the one worker who builds
his empire, Man:

we men, the Christ of tomorrow.

Pentecost
Twenty-third Sunday

> The girl is asleep, not dead.
> GOSPEL

The end of time is drawing near (the time of the rule of the powers of death). The new time has come; its king is Jesus. He sets up his administration: the disciples. They must integrate into the kingdom of life men who are still subject to the gods of the flesh, and powerless.

In his account of three vivid episodes (a father's plea on behalf of his dead daughter, the curing of a sick woman, the raising of a dead girl), Matthew indicates the conditions of incorporation in Christ. The doctrinal substance and the historical realism of the story are based on 2,000 years of Jewish history, culture, and literature. Let us get the actors and the action clear.

Actors

1 Jesus and his people, that is	2 The father and his dead daughter, that is	3 The impure sick woman, barren, excommunicated, that is
the kingdom	the first-called	the last to be called
the king	the officials	the inhabitants
Yahweh	the Jews	the Gentiles
Jesus Christ	the baptized sinners	atheists and unbelievers

1 Jesus: Lord, King, bridegroom, brother, son, sent, approved, Messias: he is there, and therefore he saves.

2 and 3 The flesh: barren, sick, dead but conscious, and asking longed-for happiness of the proper authority, God. It surrenders. God promises and does the rest.

The divine bridegroom and the daughter of nothingness (that is, the flesh, creation, the condition of being human) could be joined only after each had freely chosen the other (choice, selection, judgment). We are nearing the end of a difficult engagement. We have to realize that woman, in the Bible, represents creation confronting the Creator, the nation confronting the king. Jesus, here, shows himself to be the true father of the dead girl, the true husband of the barren woman, etc. He assumes responsibility for the health, success, fecundity, of all. Before him, the "Jairuses" brought forth "dead works" (the daughter): trees without fruit, ready to be cut down.

What makes Jesus' saving action possible?

1. The individual sufferer's appeal to Jesus: recognizing and declaring his sickness and rejecting all recourse to the unreal gods of the flesh, to the "belly-god" of today's epistle.

2. Physical contact with Jesus: today, the sacraments, Communion.

For the meaning of tassels, see Numbers 15:38–40;
on the subject of touching, see Psalm 103:32;
for the meaning of the child, see Luke 1:42.

140

Action

The King's role: to give the fullness of joy to his people.

The servants' role: to bring unhappy men to the King. In other words, not to rejoice (rise again) until everyone is present and the mission accomplished. We are to refuse rest and peace on earth. Our job is to bring to the workshop of the Kingdom those who drag themselves along in sterile anarchy and ignorance—atheists, non-practicing Christians, those who are outside Christ, outside God (the sick woman), bereft of the promises, of the gifts, of life . . . eternally.

The Bible teaches us to see the role of the older son, the first-born, the king or ruler, as being one of service to the lowest. Jesus dies for his younger brothers. Joseph's exile is to benefit his murderous brothers. Esau gives place to Jacob, his junior; Saul to his page, David. And the little dead girl, first in regard to the promise, is last to be cured. But the impure woman owes her luck to the conversion and the patience of Jairus. And Jairus owes his to his unconscious collaboration in the woman's salvation.

We are saved by saving. To save is to suffer (to give birth). Suffering = an aspect of our responsibility for those who have less experience of the faith. Before seeing his daughter come to life again, Jairus must help to heal the impure woman.

Servants of Christ, serve *now*. You'll have your fun later.
Now we must be content with *faith;*
tomorrow, the *resurrection* will fill our cup to overflowing.

This absolute victory is assured:
1. if you seek Christ, by going up to him, then walking with him, like Jairus;
2. if you recognize, acknowledge, and proclaim your weakness, giving it to Christ like the dead girl;
3. if you touch Christ through the sacraments, through Communion.

Feast of Christ the King

Thou sayest it; I am a king.

GOSPEL

Who Is Christ?
>   *For us?*

One of us. A man.

A product of our basic industry: the genetic industry of mankind.

A perfectly adjusted, perfectly selected prototype, established once and for all.

And he is the only son of God, God himself who took the flesh of our race in order to be the first man who was finished, complete, flawless.

He was offered to the Father to be tried, judged, approved: the *Passion*.

He was offered to the Father as the first fruit;

offered in thanksgiving for our appointment to the created order;

offered in thanksgiving for our appointment to the uncreated order.

He was branded (offering of our flesh, of our murderous hands);

branded by each and every believer, who in so doing, and thanks to Christ, is raised to the stewardship of the world.

143

For God?

He is the eternally finished and unique product of the divine and paternal industry. He is God's son, and he is also God: his Word. His perfect Servant. His Christ. His ambassador. His official spokesman.

God accepts him, in this human livery, as the ambassador of men, as their advocate.

He gives back to him the full powers he had before the earthly adventure. He makes him the King of Earth and Heaven. He empowers him to rule all this, along with his followers, his little brothers, for whom he claims the same privileges (Joseph and his brothers before Pharao). He conveys his decision immediately by getting things started: the *resurrection*.

For Himself?

He is responsible for the blossoming, the success, the happiness of the earth.

He has to lead every son of man to become "like" him: "Like God," said the serpent; "like Us," said God in the earthly paradise.

He has to guide the long pilgrimage, the long caravan, the long history of men. He has to bring it to God, into the "Divine Milieu," into the Divine World. He must ensure this outlet to human endeavor. He must, by definition, divinize the people of men, his younger brothers.

But all this we say every day, all over the world, in the Canon of every Mass.

First of all,
in the Preface (let's read it),
in the *Te igitur* . . .
in the *Hanc igitur* . . .
in the *Quam oblationem* . . .
And then
in the *Unde et memores* . . .
in the *Supra quae* . . .
in the *Supplices* . . .

And we say it, finally, more clearly, in a kind of summing
up, in that beautiful cry: *"Per quem . . . Per ipsum . . .":*
"It is through Christ that the Father creates, sanctifies,
vivifies, blesses the World,
and gives this World to us.
But it is also through him, in him,
by giving him to the Father,
that we, the World,
honor the Creator,
thank him,
pay homage to him and praise him."

All Saints

. . . till we have sealed the servants
of our God on their foreheads.
E P I S T L E

Let us rejoice!
Today we celebrate the feast of All Saints,
our whole parish, every lucky one of us
whose foreheads are sealed with the seal of
the Living God.

Do you have the seal? Let's see.
Fine, you can come in.
If not, go back to the factory,
because you're not under warranty,
and everyone in heaven will be distrustful of you
for all eternity.
You see, don't you? It isn't possible.
Goodbye.

Christ the Lamb never lets down
those who bear his seal.
The saints = the preserved: reserved.
The Gospels are written music.
What are saints, and what are they for?
The saints are sung music.
Without the saints, religion is flat.

When St. Augustine, bishop and doctor of the Church,
addressed his flock, he used the form:
"Your Holiness."
And the usage has survived,
but only for the Pope.

Let us deserve the title once more.

The Lord Acts

The Signs of Love

The Mass

Why do we gather together on Sunday?
So that, on the Lord's day,
the Lord should not be deprived of his members;
his body must not be scattered on that day.
Once assembled, what should we do together?
Hear the head speak,
feel the blood flowing through our arteries.

(Text dated A.D. 250)

Each week, the liturgy of the Mass
is a voyage to the end of the night,
to the frontier between two worlds,
far from the sea, far from the plain,
high up in the mountains,
along an arduous track,
in a starless night.

But you hear the guide speaking,
and you see the lights the others are carrying,
and you eat a special food.

One day we'll reach the plateau,
the summit where God dwells.

Christians are made
out of people who seek a living God.
So we talk;

151

then we sign up.
We have advanced
from the search to the word,
from the word to the sacrament.

Here is the place of assembly
of the allies of God.
The enemy is encamped all around, threatening.

Fear nothing; *he* is there.

Missing Mass is no small matter.
For if you refuse to attend the gathering,
if you do not hear the Word which explains things,
if you upset the partnership with a dubious offering,
if, having brought nothing, you take nothing away either,
you do not leave as one entrusted with a job to do,
and the *Ite, missa est* is but a sad "See you later."

To really attend Mass is no small matter.
It means moving firmly
from dispersal to assembly,
from assembly to the Word,
from the Word to personal commitment,
from personal commitment to communion in Glory,
from communion to the active service of the gods.

God calls some men up for service.
He instructs them,
and sends them out.

Those who have heard him
come,
then listen,
then work.

A Christian comes to church
to bear witness,
to commit himself publicly
in common with the body of the disciples of **Christ**,
who have died to the ways of the earth
and risen to the ways of God;
their backs are turned to the servants of the world,
their faces are turned to the servants of Christ.

If Jesus is Public Enemy Number One of the world,
the Christian is his witness for the defense, his lawyer,
his juryman.

In order to know what he believes,
the Christian each year can draw on
20 Masses explaining Christmas,
75 Masses explaining Easter,
26 Masses explaining Pentecost.

If you make use of them,
you make headway along the trail of faith.
You're a Christian.

If you don't make use of them,
you fall back, and you make others fall back with you.

The Church expects of everyone
an alert and spontaneous cooperation
by being present,
by listening,
by receiving the sacraments,
by fulfilling the mission.

And the Church has been getting this cooperation,
sometimes more, sometimes less,
for the past 2,000 years.

Every Sunday, Jesus
comes to describe to you and to construct with you
a new king,
a new people,
a new world.
He needs laborers,
he's hiring help.
Are you coming?
A man can't make the world alone;
nor can he make a world for himself alone.

Think of a Christian without Mass, without Sunday
observance, without Communion:
his faith degenerates (into a chore, a habit, a prejudice,
into expediency, or magic);
the faith of his children turns into superstition;
that of his grandchildren into hatred of these lies;
that of his great-grandchildren into folklore;

that of his great-great-grandchildren into a frank and
militant atheism.
One alone is guilty:
the Christian without Mass, without Sunday observance,
without Communion.

A feast cannot be celebrated in a hurry.
It wouldn't be a feast if it were.
We take our time.

The least conversation takes an hour.
The same for the shortest visit, conference, . . .

A twenty-minute Mass is not a Mass but a chore.

Baptism

The parents of Frederick Henry Morgan,
able and willing to assume responsibility
for the Christian upbringing and instruction of the child,
will publicly manifest this intent
by having the rites of Baptism administered to the child
on August 15, 196–, at 4 P.M.

Whoever has heard his Gospel,
believed in this Word,
been converted to it,
professed his faith in the Lord,
will receive in Baptism,
on the Lord's own sovereign authority,
remission, without judgment, of his sins,
the new life of his Spirit, in his people,
and the promise of resurrection in "glory."

Godparents,
you are answerable, before the Church,
for the genuineness of the candidate's intentions and for
his instruction.

The right to Baptism
entails for the baptized person,
or for his parents, if he is a child,
the duties of Baptism:

1. to learn the faith,
2. to live the faith,
3. to bear witness to the faith.

The sacrament of Baptism
is a rite that proclaims the faith.
It is faith which saves, not the rite.
To indulge in a rite while skipping faith
is a new religion: absurdism.
You acquire faith by "listening" to God,
in the Scriptures or in the liturgy,
and by imitating Christ's conduct.

It's not the rite that saves
but faith, conversion.
The rite is the Word; conversion is the Spirit.
What confusion arises
when "words" are no more than "noises"!

Rite and conversion are two different things.
Two parts of the sacrament,
as there are two parts in all creation:
matter and form, Spirit and Word,
the received and the given.

In view of the practice of infant
Baptism, and the absence of any well-grounded
preparation, the problems of faith
arise for each of us within the Church,
instead of arising before we come into the Church.
This situation has been troubling pastors since the
    sixth century.

Those who have heard the Word of God
desire to be baptized in the name of the Lord.
But when they recall the holiness demanded by the
    "Truth,"
they return to the rule of their evil passions.

                              (St. Justin, Second Century)

He who is converted because of a woman,
or because of a man,
or for political reasons,
or for business reasons,
is not a true convert.

                              (Ancient rabbinic text)

The man who *says:* "I believe . . . I believe . . ."
and does not *do* what I want
is not a member of the Church.

                    (Application of one of Jesus' sayings)

You wish to join the Church?
Very well.
But have you been clearly told
that the Church, at the present time, is suffering
    persecution?
You know it! In that case, come in.

The animal dies
like a rock which shatters,
but man struggles for immortality.
And one day man will triumph,
and that triumph will be Christ's day.

You who are baptized, see your opportunity.
You have been saved; become a savior in your turn.

158

You have what the world seeks; don't hide it away at the bottom of a closet.
Open up. Show it. Explain it.

You don't buy a tractor to put it in dead storage.
You don't ask for Faith to put it away;
you practice it every day,
you improve it, you cultivate it,
you show it publicly every Sunday.

To believe in Christ, the Son of God, the Saviour of the
world, is to commit oneself in practice, in reality.

Is Baptism a little party to celebrate a birth? *No!*
Baptism means being enrolled in a people who are in the
thick of action.

The infant knows nothing of this; it is up to the parents
to enlighten him. Christian parents have to educate, instruct, and train a future saint. To become holy, the child
has only to copy his parents, to listen to them.

Christian parents will therefore be the first Christians of
the parish.

Parents who refuse to observe the rules of the Church
are parents who "don't believe." They are wrong to have
their children baptized.

Christians who don't practice their religion are a little
less Christian from Sunday to Sunday and from one Easter
to the next. They make themselves incapable of seriously

teaching the Faith to their children. They deceive their children.

A good pagan is better than a bad Christian.

Christians who practice their religion get to know Christ better and better, and they have something to teach their children.

Such is the problem on which God invites you to ponder when you bring him a child to be baptized.

Because, for God, a man's baptism is a serious matter. And for Christians, their glory is to reveal to others the God they have the good fortune to know, love, and serve.

To serve God is to make him known to others, and in the first place to one's children.

That's why parents are the first whom the pastor expects at Sunday Mass and at the Communion rail; they are his principal collaborators.

If the parents waver, Baptism is a tragedy for all concerned: for the children, who will be unable to advance further; for the parents, who betray God's trust; for the Church, which has been deceived.

First Holy Communion

Before making their First Communion, everyone in our parishes is taught their catechism.
It's a big job, in preparation for a great feast.

Thank you, dear parents, for entrusting your children to me so that I may share *your work* of Christianization. I shall try to justify your trust by telling them the truth, the whole truth, and nothing but the truth.

In fact, let's begin right away, so that we know exactly where we stand, you and I.

If a youngster roams the streets without his parents, isn't he likely to get into bad company?

Don't leave your child alone on the road to God. Be at his side, searching for God. *Be with him at Sunday Mass.*

If it's good for him, then it's even better for you. If Christ spoke the truth, then you, too, should try to know what he said. If Christ is the way to eternal life, then you should take that way too.
If not, then be honest and tell the child that
it's all a pack of
idle promises,
ignorant foolishness,
incentives to laziness,
clerical fairy tales.

The sociologists tell us that *the less faith* a family has, *the more money* it spends on First Communion arrangements. And the more Christian a family, the simpler are the clothes, the gifts, the menu. Why?

The godless family adores the *image* of God—the earth; the *image* of the Holy Spirit—luxury; the *image* of God the Son—eating and drinking and making merry and talking nonsense.

So that those who love luxury drive Christ away. And those who love Christ drive luxury away. The First Communion arrangements are therefore a perfect barometer for measuring a family's religion; they make it clear to everyone what god this family really adores.

Happy the child whose First Communion is simple, unpretentious, poor, humble, quiet, for the Kingdom of Heaven is his, with its heavenly luxury—the Spirit of God.

Let the clothes the children wear, the arrangements, the decorations, all breathe the same atmosphere of simplicity and poverty.

As for a celebration afterwards, what more is needed than a family dinner, prepared with all the love and ingenuity of a mother?

Where luxury is present, the spirit of Christ is absent.

Where the Holy Spirit is present, it is useless to use luxury to compete with him.

Confession

After his threefold sin, Peter weeps.
But those tears are a "sign," a symbol, words.
They speak repentance, penance, pain, love.
That pain joins Peter to Jesus, to the Cross.
Peter, therefore, is saved, because,
being joined to Christ in death, he will also be joined
to him in the approaching Resurrection.

We re-enact these two mysteries in the liturgy:
death in *confession,* life in *Communion.*

The people of God
are a people of sinners,
people who know they are sinners.

They live only by virtue of repentance
and the pardon of the God of Mercy:
"Lord, I am not worthy . . ."

It's not new to think that everything
is someone else's fault:
the Americans blame the Russians,
the Russians blame the Americans,
the employers blame the workers,
the workers blame the employers,
the teachers blame the students,

the students blame the teachers,
the adults blame the young,
the young blame the adults,
the rich blame the poor,
the poor blame the rich.
There are only culprits.

But what is new is that
every Christian accuses himself.
Then there remains only one culprit—Christ.
That's what their leader, Jesus, thought up;
Jesus, the new Man,
the new Adam,
tomorrow's morning sun,
beneath which all will be well.

　　To sin
is to break the communion of saints.
To confess one's sin
is to break the communion of sinners.

Marriage

What happens to the young people in our parishes who get
married in church?
They were publicly united to serve Christ,
but now many of them no longer set foot in his workshop,
they no longer wish to carry the burden of the day.

On the wedding day, who was deceiving himself?
Or who was deceiving?

Science has no use for sightseeing students.
They scamp their lessons,
shirk their homework,
mess up their notes,
miss school, or come late on any pretext;
by the time they are twelve or fourteen, they have given
up any idea of progress, but they are quick to put on their
Sunday best for the prize-givings.

In the factory, it's the same; workers who just want
to sightsee are shown the door.

And it's the same in religion; there's no place for
sightseers of religious practice.
They scamp their lessons and their homework,
they shirk the Sunday gatherings,
they avoid the sacraments, prayer, witness,
they give up all practice from the time of their First
Communion,
but, for that day of public "proclamation" of their

loyalty, they were better dressed
than everyone else. . . . Ditto for marriage.

Semi-religion, semi-work, semi-science, semi-clericalism—
it's bad for everyone.
Science and faith require serious people
who learn,
who practice,
who produce,
who stand firm.
In religion, as in the factory, sightseers are dangerous to
themselves and to others.
Worse still,
they regard those who work as crazy,
and they make out that school, factory, laboratory, or
church are little more than asylums,
that students are just showing off,
workers are simpletons,
Christians are hypocrites.

All this is by way of an introduction to the story of Callista.

Callista is going to be married. She's a charming girl,
but a sightseer as far as the Faith is concerned. She hasn't
been to church for years. And Callista, who wants to get
married, wants a church wedding. Yes, a *church* wedding.

In other words, Callista wants to take advantage of
Christ toiling up to Calvary, jump up for a ride on his
cross, and "gee up!" for a little tour around the top of the
hill, have a pretty little wedding with lots of frills and

flounces and holy water and priest and bells and white dresses (the white dress of her ex-baptism and ex-proclamation of loyalty) and flowers and a nice little Mass and altar boys and confession and Communion and the whole pious works. After which, "gee up!" again on Christ's back to the church door, and you just leave me alone till my burial service. The farce is over, she jumps off the bus and turns back again into the honest little atheist she thought herself to be. So that's the story of Callista.

It's easy, Callista, to dress up in white when your parents pay for it. It's more difficult to *live in white,* under the eyes of Christ, from baptism to burial.

If you want to be honest with yourself, and with your husband and children, then be honest on your wedding day too, and get married before the magistrate.

And if you want to return to the Church, then we'll talk about it again at the proper time.

In three weeks' time . . . She has her best dress on this morning, and she knocks on the door happily.

"Come in. Why, hello, Callista. What's new?"

"Hello, Father. Well, Father, I'm getting married."

"Splendid, Callista. I'm very happy for you and for your fiancé. When is the wedding?"

"In three weeks' time."

"That's the happiest day of your life you're preparing for. You're a good housewife, Callista, you can work hard, you love children and you know how to make people happy around you."

"Yes, Father."

"Well, then, Callista, goodbye and good luck to you."

"But . . . Father . . . Don't I need papers?"

"But of course, Callista. And you must apply for them quickly at the town hall."

"And don't I need papers for the Church too?"

"For Christians, Callista, yes, I have to make out papers and other things; but unbelievers are under no obligation whatsoever toward the Church."

"But Father, I'm a Christian."

"A man isn't a general because he puts on a uniform and makes the military salute before his mirror, Callista; it's a job, a difficult one, which has to be learned and then practiced, in earnest. The same applies if you want to call yourself a Christian."

"But I have made my First Communion!"

"And what about since then? Every Sunday, publicly, you prove that you're not on Christ's side."

"I prove that?"

"You certainly do. Everything we do has a meaning. What we do is a way of saying what we are, what we think, what we believe.

"Christians, for instance, gather together to show that Christ has come, that he has a people, and that he will return to establish his rule. To gather together on Sunday is a way of inviting other people to come along, of telling Jesus Christ that we're glad it's Sunday so that we can say hello to him, learn to live like him, take his orders for the week, and work to carry out his plans for the world. So, of course, anyone who doesn't come is in fact making a public statement to the contrary. He's saying: 'Personally, I don't believe all this rubbish. I have much more important and much more interesting things to do. And anyway, my neighbors, my pals—they'd laugh at me if they saw me going to church.'

"You see, Callista, *once,* when you were twelve, you shouted very loud that you believed in Christ. But since then, fifty-two times a year, you have shouted very loud, and just as publicly, that it was Judas who was right in doing whatever he could to get rid of that muddleheaded visionary who was worth exactly thirty pieces of silver. And you're perfectly entitled to say all this, Callista, if you think it.

"Everyone knows that you have left the Church. It's what I used to teach you, at catechism: faith without works (acts) is a dead faith. Fifty-two times a year, at least, you have proved that your faith is dead. And as I have no right to take you for either a liar or a fool, I can't marry you in church."

"I can't get married, then?"

"But of course, Callista, you must get married. But you must do it at the town hall, not in church; we'd all be regarded as crazy, you, I, and all Christians. Did I ask the magistrate to ordain me a priest?"

"What will the family say?"

"Your parents don't practice any more either. So they'll be very happy if you don't have to waste your time in church on that day. They'll be happy to see that you have chosen the same road as they."

"That's true, Father, my parents don't practice any more. I don't know when my father stopped going to church, or why. As for my mother, it's since they put the new chairs in. They hurt her knees. And also she doesn't understand all the changes you've introduced; and anyways she gets churchsick—she can't stand the smell of incense . . . And then, too, she's a straightforward person, and she feels Christians go to church to show off their new hats . . . and . . ."

"That's better, Callista. I see you're beginning to laugh yourself at all these arguments. Too much proof is no proof. Maybe your mother believes all these excuses, because she'd like others to believe them, but no one else rises to the bait, not even you. You don't leave a Church you love and serve for the sake of chairs, hats, knees, and similar nonsense.

"To find the reasons why your father and mother gave up practicing, we'd have to go into the religious history of the past 150 years. And you wouldn't listen to me that long. So I'll just tell you that they followed certain trends, intellectual and emotional, without even realizing that they were trends, or whence they came, or where they were leading, or whether they were atheistic or Christian.

"Lots of false prophets turned up (as they do still), and many of their listeners were unable to distinguish between what was true and what was false in what they said (they couldn't themselves, either). So then your parents did what they found most profitable . . .

"They began by losing their faith and at the same time retaining the externals. For a virile, intelligent, and active Christianity they substituted a sort of mimicry of it, going to Lourdes for miracles, to St. Anthony for anything they

170

lost, to St. Benedict for a cure; seeking "beneficent" effects from "roses of Jericho" or glasses of Benedictine.

"But all that, Callista, is not religion.

"True religion is an ever more personal knowledge of Christ, an ever more personal endeavor, with the Church, to build up the spiritual kingdom of men.

"Your parents simply don't want the real Christ and the real Church. They have their own religion, and they don't want to purify it; they feel it's fine as it is. They don't want to know more or to see more clearly, because they think they already know everything. It doesn't occur to them to do better, because they think they are doing quite well as they are.

"With that kind of attitude, you're like a bus that imagines it has reached its destination and won't move any farther. So it is hauled off to the junk yard, where it slowly rots under the action of the sun and rain.

"That's the trouble with your parents, Callista. That's what they have been insinuating in your heart and your ears since you were quite a little girl. That's why they took you as far as your First Communion but no farther. That's why, on Sunday, when they hear the bells, they don't have time, or they don't feel well, or they don't have the right clothes, to come to church.

"That's true, isn't it, Callista? They believe in Christ only if Christ believes in them.

"But the point is that Christ wants to change them, to raise them to a new life. He wants to talk to them a lot, and give them his life through the sacraments, in an active Church.

"Your parents' religion, devoid of the Word and the sacraments, is not a budding faith but a decaying faith."

"But Father, that's the way we always learned it . . ."

Callista doesn't realize that Christ, the head of the Church, is also the head, the King, of all men, and that he is trying to rouse them all today because they were beginning to rest on their laurels in the very name of their religion.

A good officer rouses his men when they're in low spirits, dreaming of home, trying to get behind the lines, to pick up the soft jobs. They've been selected for combat duty; it's his business to put new life into them.

How does he go about it???

It's the feast of Christ the King, Callista's King. The King expects to see his officers. But Callista doesn't realize that a true princess has to be trained. And while her brothers and sisters of the royal race gather together, Callista stays in bed. What's to be done with an ill-mannered, uneducated, ignorant princess?

Two thousand years ago, the Jewish people were under Roman rule. It was no joke.

Herod, the court, the big shots, the businessmen, browbeat the ordinary folk and fawned upon the enemy for the sake of a good job or a little independence.

But the ordinary folk were buoyed up by a great hope of liberation. It wasn't an underground radio that kept up their fighting spirit but their nationalist press, read and reread and commented upon—the *Bible*.

The Bible is full of a mysterious Jewish leader who will liberate the little people, enrich the poor, bring about peace and prosperity. He is to be a son of man, of God, of David, of a virgin, a victorious warrior, an intelligent, able, just, holy founder of a stable, definitive dynasty with world-wide dominion.

We find, for instance, this:

God tells David (a simple shepherd whom he makes a king): "I shall bring the whole people back to you, as the bride returns to her husband . . ."

Two hundred years earlier, God says through Moses: "How fortunate you are, O Israel! Where else is a nation victorious in the Lord? The Lord is your saving shield, and his sword is your glory. Your enemies fawn upon you as you stride upon their heights."

And earlier still, a Jew who was enslaved and cast into prison becomes a ruler of Egypt and establishes all his brothers in the richest province of the richest kingdom.

And this nationalist press keeps harping on a single theme: If you, Israel, will return to God, God will come again to deliver you. Oh, if only it would come true, people thought! If a descendant of David would have some guts and enjoy God's favor . . .

And now here is a great prophet, beside the Jordan, talking along these lines. He's telling anyone who cares to listen to him that the time is near at hand, that the Man is ready, that the people must ready themselves in their turn. How? By penance and right conduct. And then one day he even points to a good-looking young fellow and claims that this is the strong Man, chosen by God to save his people.

The young man really is a descendant of David. Herod

tried to get rid of him by killing a bunch of babies in Bethlehem, also of the house of David. But he missed him.

Now he's about thirty years old. He's going around everywhere, waging his electoral campaign. And he's successful. He's really brilliant. It does seem that God is with him.

He keeps talking about himself, his ancestors, and God. There doesn't seem to be any way of tripping him up. He can be very stern, but also very friendly and patient. He's a marvelous speaker. But he does more than talk: he heals, multiplies loaves, wine, and fish, calms storms, cleanses the temple, forgives sins, casts out devils, acts as though he were the master of nature, of man, of society, of religion, of law. And all this with a lot of explanations of his actions, and without the slightest fear of the Romans, the Herodians, the business people, the scholars. He silences all his adversaries, one after the other.

The crowd follows, watches, cheers him.

Is he a madman? an ambitious adventurer? a genius? Is this the Man they've been waiting for, for 2,000 years, to bring peace to the world? He says yes, and he even says that he is God, and that that's what he created the world for.

On the other hand, when they want to make him a king, he slips away. He seems to have some idea at the back of his head. He's waiting for something. He proceeds very systematically. He announces that he has to be killed, to rise again, to be crowned elsewhere . . .

Those who follow him wholeheartedly trust him, listen to him, and wait. He has organized them: 12 heads of tribes, 72 auxiliaries, and a crowd of several thousand. All these people come and go from the lake, way up north, to Jerusalem, all the way south. Quite shocking, really, and so unscientific! But no one dares stop the movement or lay hands on the leader.

Our Sister Death

Dying, on the face of it, is stupid.

You die just as you are about to fall in love, or get engaged, or get married, or become a father or a grandfather, or go into retirement. It's like the abrupt stop in a miscalculation.

Death is the greatest scandal, the greatest evil, the greatest injustice.

Unless it's also a *problem* . . . You set a student a problem so that he will *think*.

On the dashboard, under the word "death," I see three levers:
1. Couldn't care less.
2. Worried.
3. Adjusted.

1. *Couldn't care less*

Whether death is a scandal, a misfortune, or an injustice, it's a fact. An unpleasant fact. And so it's rude and improper to talk about it.

The thing to do is to act as though it hadn't occurred and wasn't going to occur; as though life were a perpetual movement toward more life, youthfulness, and joy. Don't bring up a question to which there's no answer.

2. *Worried*

Death is a return to nothingness. So make the best of the good and short time you have to live. You're on a merry-go-round, and you're lucky to have hit on a good horse. Do whatever you can to stick to it. If it's a bad horse, do your best to grab a better one. Or try to manage on it. Or get off . . .

3. *Adjusted* . . . by making an effort . . . by using it

Suppose death is really just a birth? It resembles birth. It's by dying that the flower becomes seed. When a boy dies to his childhood, he is born to another youthfulness. The birth of an infant is only the passage from the mother's womb into the womb of the world. The bride leaves her home to become queen of her husband's home. The little fellow who gets off the merry-go-round when his father tells him to dies to that childhood fun, but he knows he'll have another kind of fun, later on, if he follows his father.

The Christian religion knows a man who came from God into this world in order to die to this world and to "pass" into the world of God. This man was holy even in his death. Then the Father had him sit "on his right hand," crowned him with glory and made him absolute Lord of all his possessions. He was the first man to complete the process of being born to God.

The Christian is baptized in order to be born to Christ, and the process lasts all his life; death is only the term of his Baptism, his entry into the state of Christ.

All his life, he is preparing for what must happen at his

death. When the Father calls him, he knows who it is, and why. He washes for the last time and refreshes himself for the last time at the sacraments. He bids goodbye to his brothers, and, as St. Paul says, does not grieve over it like those who have no hope.

The fatherly hand is right there, warm, firm, friendly, reassuring. And now this man can say he's born. He has left the warm maternal womb of nature. He is no longer of "father unknown." He finds he has a father whom he knows, and whose name, features, and titles he will bear from now on.

Our Friends, the Atheists

When he created humanity, God created a "community."
We are "many."
In the image of the Living God,
we are, by birth, a community of persons.
There's nothing we can do about the fact that
our personal happiness
is bound up with three billion others:
other happinesses.

The loveliness
of three billion persons, including all those who live in our
parish,
all good, strong, handsome, unique, priceless,
is at our door.
How are we to open this Ali Baba treasure cave?
That's the whole "secret" of Jesus:
love your neighbor as yourself;
do to others what you would wish them to do to you;
and let the greatest serve the lowest.
That's the aim of every effort!

When a taste for life
turns into a taste for a particular person,
it's called love.
From Jesus we know that life
is not a thing but a person,
and that person = God!

179

All honor and glory
to him who revealed this to us.

A truth which leads to contempt for people
is merely an idol.
We know that idols
demand human sacrifice:
Hitlerism, for instance, and all the nationalisms.
A truth . . . but which claims to be *the* Truth:
without charity, limit, or proportion.
The Truth,
which is not an idol but life,
is tolerant.

Our atheist friends, dear parishioners, teach us not to fool
with our faith.
We need them; let's listen to them. Without them, our
faith would not develop.
They state and explain, they represent and embody, the
hostility of the world to God; just as we state and explain,
represent and embody, the communion of the world with
the God of Jesus.

The atheists' job is to defend the integrity of the world
against all falsehood, false gods, or a true God misunder-
stood.

If God created the world, it was he who originated this
solemn confrontation; the modern atheist and also the
modern Christian have become two adults responsible for
the world.

And an adult atheism is no easier than an adult Christianity. An atheist who misunderstands Christianity is
wrong; if he misunderstands his atheism he is still more

wrong. A Christian who misunderstands the various forms of atheism is wrong; if he misunderstands his Christianity, he is still more wrong.

Issuing from the same cradle, destined to the same grave, Christians and atheists are brothers in race, in toil, and in hope. We belong to their crowd. They belong to ours.

The *truth* in whose name they oppose us lies ahead, like justice and peace. And *unity*.

For an adult Church, confrontation with atheism is not a mortal danger but an opportunity for living.

The farmer who is thinking of mechanizing his equipment doesn't only consult his neighbor who has just sold his last horse; he also checks with the man who is against mechanization.

Scientists in a laboratory who have selected one method of research also consult those who have chosen other methods.

Healthy people don't isolate themselves. They use their friends' criticisms to correct and broaden their own views.

Human friendship cannot suffer from dialogue; none of us is born just, learned, skillful, and wise.

It is humanity's job to build up *together* its joy, its prosperity, its light, its dwelling.

As long as a single one of the three billion inhabitants of the earth is absent from the council table, the biggest chunk of reality is missing from our happiness.

And here is a text for you to read carefully, dear parishioners:

". . . The Party uses the tools of ideological influence to educate men in the spirit of a *materialistic-scientific* concept of the world, in order to overcome *religious preju-dice* but without affronting the feelings of believers.

"We must patiently explain the futility of religious be-liefs, born in the past of men's subjection to the blind forces of nature, of social oppression, of the misunder-standing of the true causes of natural and social phe-nomena.

"We should base our arguments on the achievements of modern science, which gives us an ever clearer picture of the world, increases man's power over nature, and leaves no place for the fantastic *inventions* of religion concerning *supernatural* forces."

(Congress of the Communist Party, USSR)

So there's a fine challenge for the Christians of the East. And also for those of the West. In fact, for believers every-where and at all times.

For this document simply repeats, in modern language, what the serpent (symbol of the power of human reason) suggested to Eve (symbol of the earthly phase of our des-tiny) about acquiring a fruit of great price (symbol of the scientific and other knowledge required for man's full development).

We should not blame the atheistic Communists of the USSR, or other atheists, for their negative attitude to re-ligion. Under the mythological language of symbolism, the wise men of 3,000 years ago were split into the same two camps as today: believers and non-believers, scientific ma-terialists who believe in God and scientific materialists who don't believe in God.

Actually, this duality resides at the heart of every man, influencing all his thinking and doing: on the one hand, Eve, the atheist, dazzled and satisfied by the world, and Adam, the theist, feebly defending his spiritual integrity. But since the wise men of all peoples (and among them the Jewish prophets) initiated the discussion, Eve's position has been vastly strengthened; now more than ever, success seems assured: economic and psychological techniques inspire the boldest hopes in a humanity a stone's throw from political and cultural unity.

And how about Adam's position? Has that been strengthened too? Certainly, Christians—and you should know it—it is no longer the primitive Adam debating with Eve but man brought to perfection in the Spirit since Christ's baptism 2,000 years ago. That man made Eve queen of heaven, after personally meeting God at home.

It is our fault, as Christians, as Christ's disciples, if the message of the God-Man reaches our atheist friends obscured and distorted by sectarianism or by action contrary to his Spirit, emasculated by our mechanical and lifeless practices, debased by conformity, indifference, greed, and compromise with the powerful of the earth.

Atheists judge the Church by the attitudes of those who claim it as their mother. Through Christians and the Church, they see in religion an obstacle to what is most valid in their endeavors, but they can hardly see what is valid in the *"art of living by Christ,"* the Christian religion.

We are the rich farmer dozing on his neglected property.

Processions, Yesterday and Today

As the traveler walks and eats, the Christian, my dear friends, walks in procession and communicates. But his progress is not measured in miles, nor his food in calories.

Formerly
Christians came every Sunday to see the Eucharist, and partook of it once a year. And they were all the more careful and reverent in carrying the Eucharist once a year to their sick in solemn procession.

Today
Few adults take part in such processions, but our contemporary faith has rediscovered the meaning of the *Eucharistic Bread,* and with the relaxation of fasting regulations, a larger percentage than ever before of those going to Mass are receiving Communion. At the same time, the liturgy is rediscovering the wealth of meaning in processions, and is making considerable use of them. Walking is a token of commitment.

As a matter of fact,

1. Every Mass begins with a vast procession of Christians publicly leaving their earthly houses to proceed to the House of God. This is one way of proclaiming their views about the world and their *faith* in another one.

2. Every Mass ends with a vast procession of Christians returning into the world with a mission: to proclaim the Good News of Christ risen and raising all men. They real-

184

ize their responsibility toward him whose name they bear, as well as his honor and message and Body and Spirit.

3. Every Mass initiates an offertory procession in which each disciple places himself at Christ's disposal.

4. And finally, every Mass includes a Communion procession in which the disciple makes personal contact with the Master and receives from him a body which is also a duty, a power, a food, and a wage.

5. Every year, a particularly elaborate procession marks the beginning of the Palm Sunday Mass and, a week later, that of the Easter Vigil.

6. Lastly, every Burial Mass opens with a triumphant entrance procession which proclaims our unhesitating faith in the resurrection of the body through faith in Christ. And this Mass ends with a final procession out of the church in which the crowd, singleheartedly, carries the body of a member of the living Christ to his grave, so that on that day the whole earth communicates and is nourished by him who said of himself that he was "the Life."

Thus the practice of processions has developed in the Church, both in meaning and in importance, and has shifted from an annual event, festive and exceptional, to become a part of the daily liturgy.

It is to be anticipated that an increasingly conscious and widespread use of this sacred function, the religious procession, will progressively eliminate the old practice of solemn processions. The latter were more in keeping with the joyous and demonstrative piety of former centuries than with the urge to understand and to be heard, which is the glory of our own times.

It should be added that in associating the public thoroughfare with the Christian cult, the solemn processions of the past were completely in line with the medieval social structure, based on the official unity of Church and State. The civil and religious spheres were not sharply differentiated, as they are today; this differentiation is one of the great achievements of our society.

The Church

A telephone call to the rectory.

Hello? . . . your friend X is in trouble. He'd like
you to come over to his place today.

Hello? . . . yes . . . it's me.
Tell Jesus I don't have time.
Say "hello" to him from me.
Bye. Bang goes the receiver.

All right, I'll pass on the message . . .

If believers find favor with you,
O passer-by who seeks the Living God,
come in, for you're expected (gathering);
listen to the Living Jesus speak of the living you (readings);
start off toward the spiritual crossroads of the world
(offertory);
communicate in the new dimensions of the world (bread);
proclaim the news of your resurrection (dismissal).

Our mission has always been to announce Christ.
Christ is a special way
of organizing ourselves, of learning, of eating, of acting.
Our present mission is
to bring all our strength to a world
which is seeking the forms of its future real fraternity.

The twelve—*the bishops*—
gather Christ's members around their head;
they "signify" in this world
the definitive kingdom,
already "consummated" in Christ Jesus.
Without them, the Kingdom of God is only an "idea,"
a "word."

The *priest*
is the response on behalf of the man who seeks the
meaning of life;
he holds the answer for the man who is trying to put
meaning into his life.
And the priest's answer is the whole Church,
the living Church, the Church experienced.
And this Church is simply the world,
the world directed toward a father, steered by an older
brother,
directed toward God the Father, steered by God the Son,
vivified by God the Holy Spirit.
The world served by God.

The liturgy makes the spiritual world, the kingdom of
Christ, visible to the eyes of the believer.
The liturgy causes a believer to live in a life wholly
directed toward God.
The liturgy causes him to experience the meaning of life
with God.
The *liturgy* is like *nature*:
both have been concealing enormous unexploited reserves,

both have been catering to minimum needs.
But the creative youthfulness of modern man needs to
open its reserves in order to live.

Science and liturgy are both delivering their secret
treasures in answer to our thirst for more intensive living.

God

Do you owe anything to God?

I should say not! He's taken everything away from me!
I've lost money;
I've lost my health;
I've lost my wife;
I've lost my fiancé;
I've lost my child;
I've lost on all counts!
What I have, I owe it to myself alone!

Then you should not come here.

If what you have you owe to God,
then you don't owe it to the flesh.

Actually, you owe the flesh nothing.
Don't listen to it;
don't give in to it;
don't follow your instincts.
The flesh is one of God's servants—an unfaithful,
blundering steward.

The faithful steward is Christ;
it's with him you should deal.
Listen to him;
you'll find yourself better off.

The multimillionaire's bank

You owe something?
Pay up.

Someone owes you money?
Be patient.

You owe something?
Your creditor will be patient.

Be patient!
You'll get your money back.

Do as you would want others to do to you.

You owe everything to the Living God

Instinct seeks to collect your debts,
seemingly on behalf of God.
Instinct is a disloyal servant, incapable and discharged.
Don't pay.

Jesus comes on behalf of God.
He is the faithful, accredited, legitimate steward.
Deal with him confidently.
He remits debts.

By Way of Conclusion

God invented "the flesh,"
as a parent provides a nurse for his infant son.
Wasn't this enough for the time being?
It constituted the most pleasant possible earthly paradise,
enclosing you, entertaining you, accustoming you
to this present paradise.

This earthly paradise, which was sufficient then—
you've explored it twenty times—a thousand times—as a
baby explores his playpen.
(Though from cradle to playpen, what a leap to joy,
to independence, power, contact!)
Now the pen in its turn is too small for you.
The earthly paradise has bars, frontiers;
there's something beyond it.
Go, leave, rise up, cross over.
Has it roused your ambitions? Fulfill them.
Has it turned out to be a desert? Leave it.

Through the flesh, God was awakening you to yourself,
to himself, to what is of him in you. The flesh, this world,
is only as limited as you are now. It is your present, preg-
nant with your future.

Your future, son of God, is God. God is your condition.
Now the world and yourself and your power seem to you
like a prison, a desert—a call. You are ready for the definitive leap.

With St. Paul, cross over from the flesh and its laws to
the Spirit—you can do it. With Paul, lord of crime and

of the law that kills and of bloody inquisition, murderer
of the saints through supreme fidelity to the flesh and its
laws, grasp your liberty through the Spirit of God, and
with him shout what you see:

"Now the works of the flesh are manifest, which are
immorality, uncleanness, licentiousness, idolatry,
witchcrafts, enmities, contentions, jealousies, anger,
quarrels, factions, parties, envies, murders, drunken-
ness, carousings and such-like" (Gal. 5:19–21).

As a modern man, you can easily list some more up-to-
date works of the flesh—of your flesh: racial hatreds; political divisions; oppression of the weak; legalized torture on
a mass scale; the atomic bomb; exploitation not only of
poor men, but also of poor nations and poor continents;
commercialization of sex, of Faith, of beauty, of hope;
neurosis—in a word, the exasperated loneliness which
reaches for contact, communion, personal and social integrity at any price, and cannot achieve them.

Jesus, the Man of Galilee who ascended to Judea, the
Man who willed to be born and willed to die, came only
in order to break out of this dead end, to leave the disciple-
ship of the flesh and its laws, in order to fulfill himself
divinely, to reach his fullest stature. He loved this earthly
paradise. He suffered from this prison. He found the way
out to the Father. And the Father gave him the triumphant
condition of God-Man.

With him, leave the paradise of illusion and artifice.
With him, Sunday after Sunday, receive his Breath, his

Power, his Spirit, his Wisdom. He who knows where creation began also knows where it is fulfilled.

Son of God, he says, my brother, you are getting to be less and less in the dark about yourself. Rise up, go! I freely offer you my condition.

DATE DUE

GAYLORD			PRINTED IN U.S.A.